Balm.Church
THE CHURCH FOR YOU

100 BIBLE VERSES *that will* CHANGE *your* LIFE

100 BIBLE VERSES that will CHANGE your LIFE

It's Time to Encounter the Father's Love

MARK STIBBE

© Copyright 2020–Mark Stibbe

All rights reserved. This book is protected by the copyright laws of the United States of America. This book may not be copied or reprinted for commercial gain or profit. The use of short quotations or occasional page copying for personal or group study is permitted and encouraged. Permission will be granted upon request. Scripture quotations marked NIV are taken from the HOLY BIBLE, NEW INTERNATIONAL VERSION®, Copyright © 1973, 1978, 1984 International Bible Society. Used by permission of Zondervan. All rights reserved. Scripture quotations marked KJV are taken from the King James Version. Please note that Destiny Image's publishing style capitalizes certain pronouns in Scripture that refer to the Father, Son, and Holy Spirit, and may differ from some publishers' styles.

DESTINY IMAGE® PUBLISHERS, INC.
P.O. Box 310, Shippensburg, PA 17257-0310
"Promoting Inspired Lives."

This book and all other Destiny Image and Destiny Image Fiction books are available at Christian bookstores and distributors worldwide.

Cover design by: Eileen Rockwell

For more information on foreign distributors, call 717-532-3040.

Reach us on the Internet: www.destinyimage.com.

ISBN 13 TP: 978-0-7684-5156-6

ISBN 13 eBook: 978-0-7684-5154-2

ISBN 13 HC: 978-0-7684-5155-9

For Worldwide Distribution, Printed in the U.S.A.

1 2 3 4 5 6 7 8 / 24 23 22 21 20

DEDICATION

To Tim and Sue, Holly and Harriett Eldridge, and the lovely Brenda Henderson, with fondest love and profoundest gratitude. And in loving memory of Dibley.

ACKNOWLEDGMENTS

I'd like to thank Bill Williams, Larry Sparks, and all the team at Destiny Image for their invaluable support and their continuing faith in me as an author. I'd like to thank Monarch Publishers for releasing an earlier version of this title back to me so that Destiny Image could produce this dynamic new reboot. I'd also like to thank my wife Cherith for her ever-cheerful companionship and her always stimulating advice.

I'd like to thank my loving heavenly Father for His tireless and unrelenting kindness in inspiring me to write books that change people's lives. And last but by no means least, I'd like to thank my black Labrador Bella, who lies at my feet every day while I write my books, and who trots by my side as I walk and pray in the beautiful Kent countryside. The love of God and the love of a dog are truly hard to beat!

CONTENTS

Tables and Illustrations

My FATHER'S Book

Before you begin turning these pages, I'd like to tell you a story—a story that will help you understand how to read the pages to come.

In 1947, my adoptive father Philip Stibbe wrote and published his one and only book. He had been schooled well in the art of writing, having studied under C.S. Lewis at Oxford University. Dad knew how to write elegantly and clearly; Lewis mentored him well.

My father's book is called *Return via Rangoon* and it was first published just after the Second World War. It is the moving account of his time fighting in Major General Wingate's column behind enemy lines in the dense jungles of Burma. Dad was part of a special force (called the Chindits) tasked to cause as much disruption as possible. One day there was a battle in a village called Hintha and Dad was seriously wounded. A bullet went through his shoulder, just millimeters from his heart, and came out the other side.

Dad's prospects were not good. The rule was that if anyone was wounded, they had to be left behind in the jungle to fend for themselves. As a special military unit, Wingate's column had to move fast and could not be held up by caring for the injured. However, a Gurkha rifleman called Moto volunteered to stay behind, so that Dad was not left alone.

For days and days Moto looked after Dad, foraging through the local villages for food, applying fresh dressings to the wound, and fetching water. If Moto had not been there, Dad's chances of survival would have been minimal. But this selfless rifleman—a Christian from the Karen tribe—chose to remain with a wounded officer rather than stay in the greater safety of the marching column. It is hard to express how much my family owes to him.

And it is even harder when I tell you that Moto one day did not come back. Dad had seen him go off to find food and water, just like on previous days. But this time Moto did not return. Worried that something had happened, my father somehow struggled to his feet and walked toward the nearest village. As he approached its boundary, he saw to his horror that there were two enemy soldiers sitting in the clearing in the center of the village with their rifles, bayonets fixed. He knew he could not escape so he shouted as loud as he could to alert Moto to the danger.

But Moto could not hear. Later, my father discovered what had happened. Enemy soldiers had been out on patrol searching for a British officer hiding in the jungle. They were eager to interrogate him for information about Wingate's army. But instead of capturing my father, they had come upon Moto and they tortured him. Moto would not divulge the whereabouts or even the existence of my father. In the end, realizing that there was no way Moto was going to tell them anything, they shot him.

For the next two and a half years my father spent his time in jail as a POW (prisoner of war). His final place of incarceration was the notorious and horrific Rangoon jail where he was frequently questioned and tortured. He never talked about this, writing only very briefly about it in *Return via Rangoon*. But he suffered badly. Many of his friends and colleagues died of punishment, starvation, and disease.

One day in 1945, the soldiers took all the POWs out on a forced march. They told them that they were being moved to a camp. But the reality was that the Allies were advancing on Rangoon jail and the war in the Pacific was nearing its end. As the prisoners walked through the jungle, the enemy soldiers suddenly disappeared. Not long afterward, a column of Allied soldiers approached the emaciated POWs and gave them the news that they had been waiting for; they were free.

Within several weeks, my father was on a plane home, flying over England and then returning to his parents. Within months, he was back at Oxford University renewing his English degree studies. During that time, he worked on the only book he ever wrote—and what a book it is! After the Bible, *Return via Rangoon* is my most precious book. It is the beautifully written story of one man's triumph over adversity.

It may sound odd to mention the Bible and *Return via Rangoon* in the same sentence. The Bible, to be sure, is very different. It is read by millions of people all over the world. It is the best-selling book of all time. In fact, it's more than a book; it's really a library of sixty-six books covering the whole of human history, from Paradise Lost in the Garden of Eden (*Genesis*) to Paradise Regained in the Garden of the New Jerusalem (*Revelation*). None of these things can be said of *Return via Rangoon*. The Bible is quite simply unique. It is divinely inspired, and its sweep is vast.

And yet there are some important similarities. *Return via Rangoon* is my father's book. Even though my father is not with me now physically, I find that in reading its pages I can hear his voice and access his heart. Even more significantly, at the very center of his story is the most self-sacrificial act imaginable—a man who lays down his life for his friend, after being cruelly questioned and abused. *Return via Rangoon* is a wonderful and compelling story—a story of extraordinary self-sacrificial love and a story of the glorious joy of being set free.

All these things are true of the Bible too. The Bible is my Father's book. Jesus of Nazareth is the subject of the New Testament—the second half of what Christians understand to be the Bible—and one of the unique things about Him is what He revealed to us about the Father heart of God. These words from John's gospel chapter 14 verses 1–7 are a telling example:

"Do not let your hearts be troubled. Trust in God; trust also in me. In my

Father's house are many rooms; if it were not so, I would have told you. I am going there to prepare a place for you. And if I go and prepare a place for you, I will come back and take you to be with me that you also may be where I am. You know the way to the place where I am going." Thomas said to him, "Lord, we don't know where you are going, so how can we know the way?" Jesus answered, "I am the way and the truth and the life. No one comes to the Father except through me. If you really knew me, you would know my Father as well. From now on, you do know him and have seen him" (NIV).

These famous Bible verses showcase the unique revelation of God that we find in the teaching of Jesus. They reveal that the God who created the universe is a loving Father. They show that Jesus is the way to the Father,

He is the truth about the Father, and He is the life of the Father. They show that Jesus is also the *only* way to the Father—a claim that underlines the fact that there is no one like Jesus on the stage of history. He stands alone!

Jesus speaks all the time about this "Father" because "Father" is the premier name for God on His lips. Jesus called God "Father" and taught His disciples to pray "Our Father." The word He would have used is an Aramaic word, *Abba*. *Abba* is the first word uttered by many Middle Eastern children even today. It means "Daddy," and while it is a reverential term, it is the most intimate and affectionate form of address that a child can use.

And all this helps to point us to what the Bible really is, and indeed how to read it. The Bible is not really a legal book, full of rules and regulations. It is our Father's book. When we read its pages, we hear His voice and we learn more about His character. Even though we cannot see Him face to face, we can know Him personally because of Jesus.

And here's the point: like Moto, Jesus willingly gave Himself up to the most appalling suffering and death, and He did that out of self-sacrificial love so that others could be free.

Like *Return via Rangoon*, then, the Bible is a book written by an adopting father. It is a story of great love and of glorious freedom, for as Jesus said in Luke 4:18–19:

> *The Spirit of the Lord is on me,*
> *because he has anointed me to preach*
> *good news to the poor. He has sent*
> *me to proclaim freedom for the prison-*
> *ers and recovery of sight for the blind,*
> *to release the oppressed, to proclaim*
> *the year of the Lord's favor* (NIV).

In the pages that follow, I am going to be providing my top 100 Bible verses that, taken together as a continuing story, will change your life. You'll find fifty from the Old Testament and fifty from the New. In both parts, I have chosen verses that I hope and pray will enable you to hear the Father's voice and learn more about His character. I have also chosen verses that point to the big story that the Bible tells—a love story, not a law story—and that lead to the key event of the sixty-six books of the Bible, the supreme act of saving love demonstrated by Jesus' death on the Cross.

I want to encourage you to read these verses not just as ancient wisdom but also as living words from the Father's heart. Read them as words of love to you personally. Let them not only illuminate your head but also warm your heart. Let your Father reach out to you through these Bible verses and allow the Holy Spirit who inspired them to capture your heart with the Love of all loves. Whether they are written in the language of the King James Version (now 400 years old) or in the language of the New International Version (a more contemporary translation), these verses have the capacity to bring love to the unloved and hope to the hopeless. They are part of the love story of Scripture and are personal notes of affection to you.

And for a special bonus extra, at the end of this book I shall take these 100 verses and turn them into an affectionate letter from the Father to you and me *personally*. Why? I can sum it up in a single sentence.

The Bible is not meant to be read legalistically but relationally.

My prayer is that you will read the verses in this book, and the letter at the end, as a direct appeal to your heart.

My prayer is also that you will be brought to the place where you can say yes to the Father's invitation and say in the words of 1 John 3:1:

How great is the love the Father has lavished on us, that we should be

*called children of God! And that is
what we are!* (NIV)

If the entire Bible could be encapsulated in a single sentence, then it would cry out like the resounding waves of the sea, **"The Father loves you!"**

—St. Augustine

THE OLD TESTAMENT

— 1 —

*In the beginning God created the
heaven and the earth.*

Genesis 1:1 (KJV)

*In the beginning God created the
heavens and the earth.*

Genesis 1:1 (NIV)

Stories often begin with the phrase, "Once
upon a time." The Bible tells the greatest
story ever told and its sweep is immense, from
the beginning to the end of time. Instead of
starting, "Once upon a time," it opens with
the memorable words, "In the beginning God

created." The word translated "created" is a Hebrew verb (Hebrew is the language of the Old Testament) and it is only used of God's creative activity. God is the exclusive subject of this verb "create." This underlines the fact that our Father fashioned the heavens and the earth from nothing. He did this to prepare a home for human beings to inhabit, a place in which He could be our Father and we could be His children. God created the universe and planet earth out of love and for love. Creation out of nothing is a supreme miracle and an extraordinary gift. It marks the start of the love story of the Bible, a story in which our perfect Father will pursue us out of His great and infinite kindness, longing to bring us back to His arms of love.

— 2 —

And God said, Let us make man in our image, after our likeness: and let them

*have dominion over the fish of the
sea, and over the fowl of the air, and
over the cattle, and over all the earth,
and over every creeping thing that
creepeth upon the earth.*

Genesis 1:26 (KJV)

*Then God said, "Let us make man
in our image, in our likeness, and let
them rule over the fish of the sea and
the birds of the air, over the livestock,
over all the earth, and over all the creatures that move along the ground."*

Genesis 1:26 (NIV)

After creating the universe, God created
human beings. The Hebrew word for God
here is *Elohim*, and it is plural. That is why it's
followed by the statement, "Let *us* make man
in our image." A plural word is used ("us")
because the Bible uniquely reveals that the
one true God is three persons in one being.

He is triune, "three-in-one." He is Father, Son, and Holy Spirit and He created us. Human beings did not therefore gradually appear by natural, random processes. We were created. Furthermore, while fish, birds, and livestock are said to be "living creatures" (Gen. 1:20), only human beings are said in the Bible to be created "in God's image." This means that we were created to reflect God and to do what God does. God is King of creation and He authorized human beings to rule over the world in love. This does not mean domination and oppression; it means a responsible and caring oversight of the earth. This was the original mission given to us by our loving Father. We are to bring His rule to creation. We are to bring the kingdom of heaven to the whole earth.

– 3 –

*And the Lord God formed man of the
dust of the ground and breathed into
his nostrils the breath of life; and man
became a living soul.*

Genesis 2:7 (KJV)

*The Lord God formed the man from
the dust of the ground and breathed
into his nostrils the breath of life, and
the man became a living being.*

Genesis 2:7 (NIV)

The climax of God's creative work is the
forming of Adam, the first man. While everything else in creation is *spoken* into being
("And God said," Genesis 1), the first man
is *formed* by God. The word "formed" is
the same as that used for a potter forming a
pot from clay. God pressed the mud of the

ground (*adamah* in Hebrew) and formed Adam (*adam*). This is only true of Adam. And He not only *formed* Adam, He *filled* him. He breathed into Adam's nostrils. God's life force entered Adam, turning him into a living, speaking soul. This shows that the breath of God had spiritual as well as physical power. It wasn't just for human existence on the earth; it was also for intimate communion with God. You can clearly see from this that Adam is a special creation because no other creatures have the spirit of life inbreathed by God personally. Adam was created by God in a unique and intimate way. When Adam came to consciousness, he found himself face to face with his loving, heavenly Father. He found himself confronted by Love.

– 4 –

Now the serpent was more subtil than any beast of the field which the Lord

God had made. And he said unto the
woman, Yea, hath God said, Ye shall
not eat of every tree of the garden?

Genesis 3:1 (KJV)

Now the serpent was more crafty than
any of the wild animals the Lord God
had made. He said to the woman, "Did
God really say, 'You must not eat from
any tree in the garden'?"

Genesis 3:1 (NIV)

So far, so good. Except that the story now takes a turn for the worse. A demonic interloper arrives in the Garden of Eden in the visible appearance of a snake. He is identified in the New Testament as "Satan," the "Adversary" (see the Book of Revelation 12:9). Satan is the enemy of God and all things good. He was originally an angel of light called the Morning Star (or "Lucifer," which means Light-bringer). He rebelled against God and fell from heaven, taking one-third of the angels with him. After his fall, instead of retaliating directly against the Father—a fight he couldn't win—Satan took his revenge on God by tempting human beings to forsake the special relationship they had with the Father and to fall into the same orphan state that he had chosen. Tragically, our first human parents fell for the argument, "Did God really say?" From a state of primal innocence and intimacy they chose to sin. Ever since then, all have sinned and been orphaned (separated from the Father) because all are descended from this first Adam. We all derive from the son who became an orphan.

- 5 -

So he drove out the man; and he placed at the east of the garden of Eden Cherubims, and a flaming sword which turned every way, to keep the way of the tree of life.

Genesis 3:24 (KJV)

After he drove the man out, he placed on the east side of the Garden of Eden cherubim and a flaming sword flashing back and forth to guard the way to the tree of life.

Genesis 3:24 (NIV)

After creation comes catastrophe. Having created a perfect world, the Father is now compelled to banish Adam and Eve from the Garden of Eden. This may seem a very harsh act. How could a loving Father drive His children from the home that He had made for them? The answer lies in the verses leading up to this one. There the Father expresses His concern that Adam and Eve should not be left within reach of another tree in Eden, the Tree of Life. They had already disobeyed God by eating from the Tree of the Knowledge of Good and Evil. If His children now ate of the Tree of Life, a tree that conferred immortality on them, then they would be forever fallen and forever unredeemable. So, the Father quickly and decisively drives Adam and Eve out of the garden and stations *cherubim*— angelic warriors with fiery swords—to prevent re-entry. From this moment on, man will experience the hardship of toiling for a living and woman the pain of giving birth. These are the consequences of disobedience; they show how serious sin is in the Father's eyes.

— 6 —

And the Lord said unto Cain, Where is Abel thy brother? And he said, I know not: Am I my brother's keeper?

Genesis 4:9 (KJV)

Then the Lord said to Cain, "Where is your brother Abel?" "I don't know," he replied. "Am I my brother's keeper?"

Genesis 4:9 (NIV)

Having left Eden, Adam and Eve gave birth to two sons, Cain and then Abel. Abel was more devoted to the Lord than Cain and brought an offering to the Lord that pleased Him. Cain's offering, however, did not find favor with God, so Cain grew angry and downcast. God warned Cain that sin was crouching at his door and desired to master him. But Cain gave in to sin and killed his brother Abel.

It is at this point that God appears and asks Cain where Abel is. Cain responds sarcastically and defensively. But he cannot hide from his Father and he is now condemned to be "a restless wanderer on the earth." Here, the very next chapter after the fall of Adam and Eve, we see sin taking hold of humanity. Instead of behaving like a spiritual son, Cain behaves like a spiritual orphan. He is angry, sad, suspicious, jealous, and consigned to a life of striving, loneliness, and fear—all symptoms of the orphan heart. Cain is a tragic example of the consequences of the fall. Humans were created to be sons and daughters but are now living like orphans and slaves.

– 7 –

I do set my bow in the cloud, and it shall be for a token of a covenant between me and the earth.

Genesis 9:13 (KJV)

I have set my rainbow in the clouds,
and it will be the sign of the covenant
between me and the earth.

Genesis 9:13 (NIV)

Many generations after Adam and Eve, humanity has degenerated into extreme corruption and darkness. Only one man, Noah, is righteous on the earth. God's Spirit says, "Enough is enough," and Noah is told to prepare an ark because God is sending a great flood to destroy the earth. Noah and his family escape the flood by sailing in a huge seagoing vessel full of living creatures. After they have landed and started out afresh, God comes to Noah with a covenant. A covenant is a promise or contract made by God with human beings. This is the first of five major covenants in the Bible. God designates the rainbow as a perpetual sign of the covenant to remind us that He will never again destroy the earth by flooding it. This covenant is for all people and it foreshadows the future work of His Son, Jesus Christ. Just as Noah's family found rescue from the flood by sheltering in the ark, so all who take refuge in Christ will be rescued from the consequences of sin. The ark is a perpetual reminder that the Father's mercy triumphs over His judgment.

— 8 —

And I will make of thee a great nation, and I will bless thee, and make thy name great; and thou shalt be a blessing.

Genesis 12:2 (KJV)

I will make you into a great nation and I will bless you; I will make your name great, and you will be a blessing.

Genesis 12:2 (NIV)

Abraham is one of the three patriarchs (leading fathers) in the Father's story. These three great patriarchs are Abraham, Isaac, and Jacob. God chooses Abraham and calls him to leave his father's house and go to a country that He will show him. Abraham shows great faith when he obeys this call. Faith is about believing that something is so, even though you cannot yet see it. Abraham believes that there is a country ahead and sets out to find it. It is on the journey that the Father speaks to him and tells him that He is going to make a great nation out of Abraham's offspring. The nation in question is Israel. Through this nation, the Father promises to bless every nation on the earth. After Abraham and Sarah have their son Isaac, Isaac later has a son called Jacob. Jacob is renamed Israel and has twelve sons who become the fathers of the twelve tribes of Israel. God is a Father who loves to bless us, and He has chosen Israel to be the nation that brings His blessing to the world. Have you ever experienced the Father's blessing?

– 9 –

*And God said unto Moses, I Am That
I Am: and he said, Thus shalt thou say
unto the children of Israel, I Am hath
sent me unto you.*

Exodus 3:14 (KJV)

*God said to Moses, "I am who I am.
This is what you are to say to the Israelites: 'I am has sent me to you.'"*

Exodus 3:14 (NIV)

Joseph, one of Jacob's twelve sons, is sold
into slavery in Egypt, but because he has the
gift of interpreting Pharaoh's dreams, he is
given a prominent position in that country.
The rest of Joseph's family eventually joins
him in Egypt, and the descendants of Jacob
(also known as Israel) live there for the next
400 years. It is at the end of that time that

the Israelites become very numerous in Egypt and Pharaoh makes them slaves. God raises Moses—an orphan child—to be the liberator of Israel. Moses' calling as Israel's deliverer comes in Exodus chapter 3 when he hears God speaking to him from a burning bush. God reveals His name, "I AM THAT I AM" (*Yahweh* in Hebrew, "Jehovah" in English). This name is almost untranslatable and is regarded as utterly sacred. It means something like "Forever" or "Always." Here God tells Moses to go to Pharaoh and to tell him, "The One who is forever has sent me to you." Never forget, your loving, heavenly Father is a forever Father. He was your Dad yesterday, yes, and today. But He is also your Dad for all eternity.

— 10 —

And thou shalt say unto Pharaoh, Thus saith the LORD, Israel is my son, even my firstborn.

Exodus 4:22 (KJV)

Then say to Pharaoh, "This is what the LORD says: Israel is my firstborn son."

Exodus 4:22 (NIV)

Before Moses leaves the desert of Midian (where he has encountered the burning bush), God tells him what to say to Pharaoh. He tells Moses to inform Pharaoh that Israel is "His firstborn son." What is very telling about this statement is that God clearly indicates here that He has a Father-son relationship with His people, the Israelites. Just as Moses was adopted by a princess, Israel was adopted by the King of Kings. God has *adopted* Israel as His very own out of all the peoples of the earth. What a privilege! Through Moses, God now tells Pharaoh to let His *son* go and uses ten plagues as a warning. Pharaoh, because of his hard heart, refuses to listen, so his firstborn son and the firstborn sons of Egypt are killed by the Angel of Death on the eve of the exodus (the great escape from Egypt). Just as Pharaoh had punished God's firstborn son (Israel), so now God punishes Egypt's firstborn sons. A national crime is met by a national judgment. God regards Israel as His son and is justly angry with Pharaoh for turning His son into a slave.

– 11 –

Now therefore, if ye will obey my voice indeed, and keep my covenant, then ye shall be a peculiar treasure unto me above all people: for all the earth is

mine: and ye shall be unto me a king-
dom of priests, and an holy nation.

Exodus 19:5–6 (KJV)

Now if you obey me fully and keep
my covenant, then out of all nations
you will be my treasured possession.
Although the whole earth is mine, you
will be for me a kingdom of priests and
a holy nation.

Exodus 19:5–6 (NIV)

Three months after the exodus (the great escape) from Egypt, the Israelites arrive at the Desert of Sinai. The people camp in front of the mountain (Mount Sinai), and Moses goes up to meet with God. There, God instructs Moses to go back down the mountain and tell the people about the covenant He has made with them. This covenant (the Mosaic covenant, the second covenant in the Bible) is an agreement between God and His people in which God promises to bless them, provided they obey His commandments. Moses tells the people that if they do that, they will be the Father's treasured possession and a kingdom of priests, a holy nation. The phrase "kingdom of priests" is especially important. The word "priest" here is *cohen* in Hebrew and it literally means "one who draws near." The Father longed for a kingdom of people who would draw near to Him in love. His heart has always desired intimacy with His people. His heart aches for this to this day. He wants to be a Dad to you and me. He wants us to revel in the knowledge that we are chosen, treasured, loved.

– 12 –

Thou shalt have no other gods before me.

Exodus 20:3 (KJV)

You shall have no other gods before me.

Exodus 20:3 (NIV)

The people of Israel have stopped at Mount Sinai, and Moses once again climbs the mountain to meet with the Father. He is given the Ten Commandments on two tablets of stone. These commandments in summary say this: God's people are to put Him first, avoid idolatry, not take His name in vain, keep the Sabbath, and honor their parents (commandments 1–5). They are also to refrain from murder, adultery, stealing, slandering their neighbor, and coveting what belongs to someone else (commandments 6–10). These are the Father's abiding guidelines for His children, if we want to live life in all its fullness and be truly, deeply happy. These Ten Commandments are therefore designed not to punish God's people but to protect them. These are the boundaries that a loving Father has established for His children. They are also the terms of the covenant with Moses. The first covenant with Noah in Genesis 9 was for everyone. This covenant is for Israel. If the people of Israel obey the covenant, then they will be blessed by their Father in heaven. They will enjoy the glorious privileges of being loved by the greatest Dad in the universe.

The Ten Commandments[1]

– 13 –

And the LORD passed by before him, and proclaimed, The LORD, The LORD God, merciful and gracious, longsuffering, and abundant in goodness and truth.

Exodus 34:6 (KJV)

And he passed in front of Moses, proclaiming, "The LORD, the LORD, the compassionate and gracious God, slow to anger, abounding in love and faithfulness."

Exodus 34:6 (NIV)

Moses continues to lead God's people as they travel toward the Promised Land. After the people rebel against God by constructing a golden calf to worship (in direct defiance of God's commandments), God tells Moses that

He has now had enough of this rebellious, orphan behavior and He now wants to leave His people. But Moses pleads with God, and God relents, saying that He will still travel with them to the Promised Land. "My Presence will go with you," He says (Exod. 33:14). Moses presses in and prays, "Show me your glory" (Exod. 33:18). God agrees to this request and allows Moses to hide in the cleft of a rock and to see all His goodness pass before his eyes. Now, in this magnificent statement from Exodus 34, we see some of the qualities of the Father's majestic glory and goodness: mercy, grace, patience, love, and faithfulness. Sometimes it is said that the Old Testament reveals a God of anger, the New a God of love. This verse shows us that there is grace and love in the Old Testament revelation of God as well. He has always been, and forever will be, a good, good Father.

– 14 –

For thou shalt worship no other god:
for the LORD, whose name is Jealous,
is a jealous God.

Exodus 34:14 (KJV)

Do not worship any other god, for the
LORD, whose name is Jealous, is a
jealous God.

Exodus 34:14 (NIV)

This verse comes at the end of the passage in Exodus 34, which begins with God saying to Moses, "I am making a covenant with you." A covenant is a lawful agreement. God's side of the contract is to protect and provide for His children in miraculous ways and to drive out the opposing tribes and nations that Israel confronts. Israel's side is to obey everything that God has commanded them. This includes the Ten Commandments in Exodus 20 and all the other laws you can find in Exodus, Leviticus, Numbers, and Deuteronomy (other Old Testament books attributed to Moses). It especially includes the command not to adopt the idolatrous practices of the pagan nations that Israel meets both on the way to and on arrival in the Promised Land. Israel is to destroy the pagan altars and to worship Yahweh alone, for the Father is jealous for His relationship with Israel, His firstborn son. Our Father is a jealous Dad. He is not jealous in some toxic, selfish way. He is jealous in a holy, loving way. He longs and aches for us to have an exclusive relationship with Him. This means having no other gods, no other idols, no other objects of worship, save Him.

– 15 –

*The LORD make his face shine upon
thee, and be gracious unto thee.*

Numbers 6:25 (KJV)

*The LORD make his face shine upon
you and be gracious to you.*

Numbers 6:25 (NIV)

This verse records a blessing to be given
by Aaron, who was Moses' assistant and the
father of a line of priests known as the Aaronic
priesthood. This is the oldest blessing in the
world, and it is also the most beautiful. Here
the Father says He will bless and keep (in the
sense of preserve) His people. He will make
His face shine upon them like the light of a
new day dawning. His thoughts toward them
will be thoughts of grace—of love that's rich
yet undeserved. He will lift His face toward

His children and He will grant them peace. The word "peace" is the Hebrew word *shalom*, and it denotes well-being, wholeness, completeness, and welfare. Its scope includes our relationship with God, with others, with ourselves, and with the world. In the Gospels, Jesus often says, "Peace be to you," which is a common greeting in Hebrew—*shalom aleichem*. Numbers 6:24–26 is truly the greatest of blessings. It showcases the length and breadth of the Father's blessing, a blessing that encompasses the whole of our lives. What a great and glorious Father we have!

– 16 –

*And in the wilderness, where thou hast
seen how that the LORD thy God bare
thee, as a man doth bear his son, in
all the way that ye went, until ye came
into this place.*

Deuteronomy 1:31 (KJV)

*There you saw how the LORD your
God carried you, as a father carries
his son, all the way you went until you
reached this place.*

Deuteronomy 1:31 (NIV)

Deuteronomy is the fifth book of the Old
Testament and in Hebrew is called *Devarim*,
the Words. Most of it consists of three ser-
mons that Moses preaches as he reviews the
previous forty years of wandering in the desert
(see Deut. 1:1–4:43; 4:44–28:68; 29:1–30:20).

The people of Israel are poised to enter the Promised Land, and Moses uses this opportunity to remind them about what God has done for them and what they themselves have done in return. Much of it contains details of the law code that Israel must live by when entering the land. Here, in this memorable verse, Moses reminds the people of God's faithfulness in the past, using the powerful picture of a father carrying his young son on his shoulders. Yahweh is the transcendent and majestic King of the universe. But He is also a caring and involved Father who nurtures, protects, and carries His children. He carried His people on His shoulders in the past. He will carry you on His shoulders in the future. He is the most adoring, doting, affectionate of all fathers.

– 17 –

Hear, O Israel: The LORD our God is one LORD.

> Deuteronomy 6:4 (KJV)

Hear, O Israel: The LORD our God, the LORD is one.

> Deuteronomy 6:4 (NIV)

Another commandment that forms part of the covenant between God and His people is this famous statement known as *Shema Yisrael*, which translated from the Hebrew means "Hear, O Israel." This declaration twice uses the word *Yahweh*, rendered as "LORD" in English. Devoted Jews will not speak the name Yahweh out loud and tend to replace it with *Adonai* ("Lord") when speaking or praying out loud, and with the letters *YHWH* (the Tetragrammaton, as it is called) when writing down God's name. The *Shema* is important because it says that God is "one." The word in Hebrew is *echad*, which means either the number one or alone. This highlights what's called the monotheistic nature of Judaism. In other words, it confirms that there is one God, not many gods, and that this God is one being. Interestingly, the word translated "our God" (in the phrase "the LORD our God") is from the Hebrew word *Elohim*, which is a plural word. So even within the *Shema*, God is telling us that He is one being, yet He is also three persons in one being, as the New Testament will show. He is Father, Son, and Holy Spirit.

– 18 –

Be strong and of a good courage; be not afraid, neither be thou dismayed: for the Lord thy God is with thee whithersoever thou goest.

Joshua 1:9 (KJV)

Be strong and courageous. Do not be terrified; do not be discouraged, for the Lord your God will be with you wherever you go.

Joshua 1:9 (NIV)

After the first five books of the Bible—Genesis, Exodus, Leviticus, Numbers, and Deuteronomy—comes the Book of Joshua. At the end of Deuteronomy, Moses dies before the people have entered the Promised Land. Moses has laid his hands upon his spiritual son Joshua, and Joshua had been filled with God's spirit of wisdom. The people therefore listen to him and he becomes their leader. In Joshua chapter 1 the Lord tells Joshua that Moses is now dead and that it is time to enter and conquer Canaan, the Promised Land. There will be many battles and trials ahead, but the Lord tells Joshua to be strong and courageous and not to fear—words that have been a source of great encouragement to many believers since. Joshua takes heart and leads the tribes of Israel into the land. Joshua's name means "salvation" in Hebrew. Joshua's story in broad outline foreshadows Jesus' story. Jesus' name also means "salvation." Jesus will show us how we can be rescued from slavery to sin and how we can live in the Promised Land of the Father's love. So, be strong and courageous. Make your own journey from fear to love.

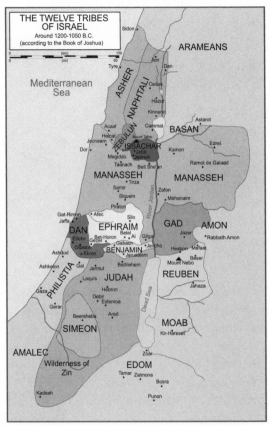

The following text labels appear on the map:

THE TWELVE TRIBES
OF ISRAEL
Around 1200-1050 B.C.
(according to the Book of Joshua)

0   (km)   100
0   (mi)   60

Mediterranean
Sea

Sidon

ARAMEANS

Tyre

Iion

Dan

ASHER

NAPHTALI

Cedes

Hazor

Kinneret

ZEBULUN

Acsaf

Helcat

Cammat

BASAN

Astarot

Jocneam

Mount Tabor

ISSACHAR

Dor

Megiddo

Jafiti

Jezreel

Kamon

Edrei

Taanach

Beit She'an

Ramot de Galaad

MANASSEH

Tirza

MANASSEH

Samir

Zafon

Siquem

Mahanaim

Piraton

Gat-Rimon

Afec

Silo

Jaffa

Betel

Ai

EPHRAIM

GAD

AMON

DAN

Elteke

Bet-Horon

Gezer

Gabaon

Gilgal

Jericho

Jazer

Rabbath Amon

Ashdod

Gibeta

Ekron

BENJAMIN

Jerusalem

Hesbon

Mefaat

River Jordan

Beser

Ashkelon

Gat

Bethlehem

Mount Nebo

Jarmut

REUBEN

PHILISTIA

Laquis

JUDAH

Gaza

Hebron

Jahaza

Gerar

Debir

Estemoa

Arad

Beersheba

MOAB

SIMEON

Kir-Hareset

AMALEC

Zoar

Wilderness of
Zin

EDOM

Tamar

Zalmona

Bosra

Kadesh

Punon

Dead Sea

Canaan and the Twelve Tribes of Israel (Joshua 14)[2]

– 19 –

And the angel of the LORD appeared unto him, and said unto him, The LORD is with thee, thou mighty man of valour.

Judges 6:12 (KJV)

When the angel of the LORD appeared to Gideon, he said, "The LORD is with you, mighty warrior."

Judges 6:12 (NIV)

After Joshua dies, a period of Israel's history begins in which God's people are oppressed by other tribes. This era is described in the Book of Judges. The reason why Israel is so frequently attacked is because God's people fail to obey the command to drive out all the other inhabitants of the Promised Land. This disobedience leads to disaster. Whenever

Israel is under the hammer during these seasons of catastrophe, God raises up judges—Spirit-empowered leaders who deliver Israel from oppression. One of the twelve deliverers is Gideon. When the Israelites are reduced to hiding in the mountains, the angel of the Lord comes to Gideon. As Gideon himself confesses, he is the youngest son of a family that belongs to the weakest clan in Israel. But the Lord sees him differently; He sees him as a mighty man of valor. How often in the Bible the Father uses weak people to defeat the strong! In His hands, ordinary people achieve extraordinary things. Never forget: God is a Father who loves to take hold of insignificant people and give them a significant purpose. This includes you and me because He is the world's greatest Dad!

The Twelve Judges of Israel

Name	Tribe	Oppressed by	Reference
Othniel	Judah	Mesopotamia 8 yrs. Opp 40 yrs, P	Judg. 3:7-11
Ehud	Benjamin	Moabites 8 yrs. Opp 40 yrs, P	Judg. 3:12-30
Shamgar	Judah	No details	Judg. 3:31
Deborah/ Barak	Ephraim/ Naphtali	Canaanites 8 yrs. Opp 40 yrs, P	Judg. 4:1-5:31
Gideon	Manasseh	Midianites 7 yrs. Opp 40 yrs, P	Judg. 6:-8:35
Tola	Issachar	23 yrs, P	Judg. 10:1-2
Jair	Gad	22 yrs, P	Judg. 10:3-5
Jephthah	Gad	Ammorites 6 yrs, P	Judg. 10:6-12:7
Ibzan	Judah	7 yrs, P	Judg. 12:8-10
Elon	Zebulun	10 yrs, P	Judg. 12:11-12
Abdon	Ephraim	8 yrs, P	Judg. 12:13-15
Samson	Dan	Philistines 40 yrs. Opp 20 yrs, P	Judg. 13:1-16:31

Key: Opp = Oppressed   P = Peace   yrs. = Years

– 20 –

*And the Lord came, and stood, and
called as at other times, Samuel, Samuel. Then Samuel answered, Speak; for
thy servant heareth.*

1 Samuel 3:10 (KJV)

*The Lord came and stood there, calling
as at the other times, "Samuel! Samuel!" Then Samuel said, "Speak, for
your servant is listening."*

1 Samuel 3:10 (NIV)

The period of the Judges comes to an
end with the birth of Samuel. Eli—who is a
priest—is mentoring the boy Samuel at Shi-
loh, the religious capital of Israel. Samuel is
the first of the major biblical prophets and
his name means "heard of God." In 1 Samuel
chapter 3 we see Samuel being woken up in

the night by a voice calling his name. He is probably around thirteen years of age at the time. Three times Samuel gets up and goes to Eli and wakes the priest, thinking that it is Eli calling him. Eli eventually realizes what is going on and tells Samuel what to say. The fourth time God calls, Samuel tells him, "I am listening." He then receives his first prophecy—a judgment against Eli, his spiritual father, and Eli's rebellious sons. The chapter ends with Eli demanding that Samuel tell him what the Lord has said and Samuel agreeing. This is a lasting lesson for all of us: if we claim to be the children of God but we behave like orphans (i.e. rebelliously), we cannot expect God to let this go. The best dads discipline their children. God, the perfect Father, is no exception.

The Lord seeth not as man seeth; for man looketh on the outward appearance, but the Lord looketh on the heart.

1 Samuel 16:7 (KJV)

The Lord does not look at the things man looks at. Man looks at the outward appearance, but the Lord looks at the heart.

1 Samuel 16:7 (NIV)

By now the age of the Old Testament Judges has all but ended and the people of Israel now ask for a king. Samuel is furious because he knows that God alone is King. God, an ever-patient Father, tells him to grant their request and Samuel anoints Saul as the first king of Israel. However, Saul's kingship is a failure, so a young boy called David is raised up to succeed Saul. The prophet Samuel is called by God to go to the house of Jesse (the father of the future King David), and seven sons of Jesse are brought before him. All of them are able candidates to succeed Saul as king, but none of them is the one. Samuel says that the Lord is not impressed by how we look on the outside but looks upon our hearts. Unlike the world, with its cult of celebrity, our Father is more interested in internal virtue than external prowess. Then the youngest, David, is brought from the hills where he has been looking after the sheep. He is the one, and Samuel anoints him for kingship, whereupon David is filled with the Holy Spirit. Samuel retires to Ramah, where he eventually dies. David, the Father's choice, begins his season of preparation.

– 22 –

*I will be his father, and he shall be my son:
and I will not take my mercy away from
him, as I took it from him that was before
thee: but I will settle him in mine house
and in my kingdom for ever: and his
throne shall be established for evermore.*

1 Chronicles 17:13–14 (KJV)

*I will be his father, and he will be my
son. I will never take my love away
from him, as I took it away from your
predecessor. I will set him over my
house and my kingdom forever; his
throne will be established forever.*

1 Chronicles 17:13–14 (NIV)

David does not become king straight
after Samuel has anointed him. He spends a
season waiting. When Saul eventually dies,

David becomes king. Later, when David has established Jerusalem as the capital city, he longs to build a Temple for God's presence there. But Nathan the prophet has a dream and hears the Lord saying that David is not the one to build Him a house. David's son Solomon is the one. The Lord also promises that He will be Solomon's Father and that Solomon will be His son and that He will always love him. Solomon, the son of David, will have a throne that will be established forever. This is God's covenant with David. Indeed, one day, Jesus of Nazareth will be born from the line of David and He will be called by many, "Son of David." He will be the King of Kings and His kingdom will be everlasting. He will be the Messiah, the anointed one, from the line of the kings of Judah, beginning with David. You can see from this how special David was to God. Despite his mistakes, David was a man after the Father's heart.

Old Testament Covenants

The Covenant with Noah
Genesis 6-18, 9:9-17
For all the people of the earth
Unconditional (i.e. not dependent on our obedience)
The sign is the rainbow

The Covenant with Abraham
Genesis 12, 15:18-21, 17:1-14
For Abraham and his decendants
Conditional (on Abraham's obedience, and that of his descendants)
The sign is circumcision

The Covenant with Moses
Exodus 19-24
For the nation of Israel (Exodus 16:1-6)
Conditional on the nation's obedience
The sign is the Sabbath

The Covenant with David
2 Samuel 23:5
For David and David's descendants
Conditional (dependent on David and his descendants' obedience)
No sign for this covenant

– 23 –

*Surely goodness and mercy shall fol-
low me all the days of my life: and I
will dwell in the house of the LORD for
ever.*

Psalm 23:6 (KJV)

*Surely goodness and love will follow
me all the days of my life, and I will
dwell in the house of the LORD forever.*

Psalm 23:6 (NIV)

King David was a great composer of
psalms, or what in Hebrew are called
the *tehilim*—praises. Psalm 23 is directly
attributed to David, as are most of the first
forty-one Psalms. Psalm 23 begins with the
well-known words, "The Lord is my Shepherd"—a title that David used because of his
own early career as a shepherd, before he was

anointed by Samuel to become king. David celebrates the Lord's pastoral care in making him lie down in green pastures, leading him beside still waters, restoring his soul, guiding him down right paths, and comforting him in the valley of death. He then praises God for preparing a feast for him and anointing his head with oil, and for filling his cup with overflowing abundance. In the final verse he gives thanks that he is pursued by God's goodness and kindness (*hesed*) and that he will dwell forever in the Father's house. It is hard to imagine a greater celebration of the Father's role as intimate provider and protector than this. David knew the Father's heart like no other person in the Old Testament, and he turned all this into song.

– 24 –

*When my father and my mother for-
sake me, then the Lord will take me up.*

Psalm 27:10 (KJV)

*Though my father and mother forsake
me, the Lord will receive me.*

Psalm 27:10 (NIV)

This is one of the most beautiful verses in
the entire Bible. Here King David gives praise
for the fact that while human beings may
abandon us, our Father in heaven is always
there for us and ready to welcome and hold
us. Notice that David speaks about earthly
fathers and mothers here. He acknowledges
that they are far from perfect. Some even forsake or desert their children. The word "forsake" is a Hebrew word that David has already
used in Psalm 9:9–10: "The LORD is a refuge

for the oppressed, a stronghold in times of trouble. Those who know your name will trust in you, for you, LORD, have never *forsaken* those who seek you." In Psalm 27 David follows the same line of thought. First, he asks the Father not to hide His face from him, not to forsake or reject him. Second, he makes the great declaration in verse 10: "Though earthly fathers and mothers may walk out on me, my heavenly Father will always be there for me." How our fatherless (and increasingly motherless) world needs to hear this today! God is a Father who even loves us in a motherly way when we need that (see Isa. 66:13). He makes up the love-deficit from our mums and dads. What a good, good Father He is!

– 25 –

A father of the fatherless, and a judge of the widows, is God in his holy habitation.

Psalm 68:5 (KJV)

A father to the fatherless, a defender of widows, is God in his holy dwelling.

Psalm 68:5 (NIV)

Way back in the time of Moses, God had made it clear that He has a special concern for two groups of people: those who have lost their fathers and those who have lost their husbands (see Exod. 22:22). There is something about these two groups of people that evokes special compassion from the Father's heart. In the Old Testament, orphans are mentioned forty times, widows fifty-six times. The phrase "orphans and widows" occurs thirty times. Here in Psalm 68 King David makes the cause of the orphan and the widow the focus in verse 5. He gives praise that God loves those who have lost fathers and those who have lost husbands. He highlights that God is present in love for both groups in His holy dwelling (a word used for the tabernacle, the tent in the wilderness, and the Temple). In this world where there are more fatherless people than ever, there is a pressing need to rediscover this expression of the Father's merciful heart. We cannot claim to be champions of the Father's love, and of the love of the heavenly Bridegroom Jesus, if we are not also champions of those who have lost fathers and husbands.

– 26 –

Like as a father pitieth his children, so the Lord pitieth them that fear him.

Psalm 103:13 (KJV)

As a father has compassion on his children, so the Lord has compassion on those who fear him.

Psalm 103:13 (NIV)

Psalm 103 is one of the most famous of David's psalms. It is full of memorable lines: "The LORD is compassionate and gracious, slow to anger, abounding in love" (verse 8). "As far as the east is from the west, so far has he removed our transgressions from us" (verse 12). But one of the most powerful verses of all is the one here, which underlines God's fatherly care for those who "fear him." The word "fear" is widely misunderstood.

Legalistic people use the word "fear" in order to enforce control over others. But "fear" is not a toxic word, denoting abusive rage. God, after all, is a Dad who is "slow to anger," "rich in love"! No, "fear" is a word full of emotional health. The verb is used three times in this psalm and it really denotes an absolute reverence for a good, good Father who knows what's best for us, and who would much rather shower us with His compassion than discipline us with His love. God is a mighty, royal Father—the greatest Father in the universe. As such, He is to be respected. At the same time, not only is He worthy of our holy reverence, He is worthy of our affection. God is a Father who evokes holy fear. But He is also a Father who has loving compassion on His children. David truly knew the heart of God!

I will praise thee; for I am fearfully and wonderfully made: marvellous are thy works; and that my soul knoweth right well.

Psalm 139:14 (KJV)

I praise you because I am fearfully and wonderfully made; your works are wonderful. I know that full well.

Psalm 139:14 (NIV)

Psalm 139 is one of the most intimate of the psalms that David composed. The overriding theme of the song is David's praise for the Father's personal interest in every aspect of his life. From his mother's womb onward, God has been watching over King David's life. Here the Father's omniscient (all-knowing, verses 1–6), omnipresent (verses 7–12), omnipotent (all-powerful, verses 13–15) nature is exalted in the most sublime poetic language. This is more extraordinary when you realize that David was writing in the context of wicked accusers (verses 19–22). It is one thing to praise God in the sunshine. It is another thing altogether to sing about Him in the rain! However, David knows that whatever people may say about God, and whatever they may say about us, God knows us, watches over us, guards and guides us like a perfect Father. In verses 13–16 David even describes God as a weaver who carefully creates the intricate tapestry of our lives. We are indeed fearfully and wonderfully made by the hands of the world's greatest Father. From the womb to the tomb, our Father invests in our lives personally.

− 28 −

*Give me now wisdom and knowledge,
that I may go out and come in before
this people: for who can judge this thy
people, that is so great?*

2 Chronicles 1:10 (KJV)

*Give me wisdom and knowledge, that
I may lead this people, for who is able
to govern this great people of yours?*

2 Chronicles 1:10 (NIV)

After David's death, Solomon succeeds his father as king of Israel. He goes to Gibeon, where the bronze altar that Bezalel had made in Moses' day is located. There he offers a thousand burnt offerings. That night, the Lord appears to him in a dream and tells him to ask for whatever he wants. This is the dream of all dreams. Solomon can have anything in the whole world. What would you have asked for? King Solomon asks for *wisdom* and *knowledge* to lead God's people. What a great request! All leaders, in whatever sphere, should ask for these two essential qualities. And God grants Solomon his prayer, because His son has not asked for money and fame, for victory over his enemies, or for a long life. He has asked for something worthy of a great leader. From Gibeon, Solomon returns to Jerusalem to reign in Israel. Shortly afterward he starts to construct the Temple in Jerusalem, the dream that his father David had. What a lesson this is! Those who are truly sons and daughters of the Father do not covet income and influence. They seek out the Father's wisdom and knowledge, which is far more precious than silver and gold.

− 29 −

*Trust in the Lord with all thine
heart; and lean not unto thine own
understanding.*

Proverbs 3:5 (KJV)

*Trust in the Lord with all your heart and
lean not on your own understanding.*

Proverbs 3:5 (NIV)

The Book of Proverbs comes from a section of the Old Testament known as "The Writings." The original title for this book in the Hebrew Bible is "The Proverbs of Solomon," indicating its author. Proverbs chapter 3 begins with Solomon saying to the one he is mentoring, "My son, do not forget my teaching, but keep my commands in your heart, for they will prolong your life many years and bring you prosperity" (verses 1–2). Here

Solomon urges his son to hold fast to the *torah*, a word which means divine instruction and direction and is often translated "Law." The son is to maintain a life of spiritual devotion by writing this teaching on his heart. He is also to put his trust in the Lord. The word means literally that he is to throw himself upon the Lord. He is not to rely on his own intellectual understanding but build his life on the Father's *hokma*, or wisdom. Those who are truly the sons and daughters of God relish their heavenly Father's words of instruction. The Bible is their favorite book. They read it regularly and lovingly. Its words are written on their hearts. Its light directs their paths in all matters.

*Many waters cannot quench love,
neither can the floods drown it: if a
man would give all the substance of
his house for love, it would utterly be
contemned.*

Song of Songs 8:7 (KJV)

*Many waters cannot quench love; rivers cannot wash it away. If one were
to give all the wealth of his house for
love, it would be utterly scorned.*

Song of Songs 8:7 (NIV)

The Song of Songs is a book also known
as the Song of Solomon. There are two main
characters in the poem: the woman and the
man who loves her. There is also a group of
onlookers called "the daughters of Jerusalem." The Song of Songs is accordingly a

collection of Hebrew love poems attributed to King Solomon. It portrays the journey of love from courtship to consummation. This book of the Bible has often been regarded as an allegory of God's relationship with Israel and Christ's relationship with His Bride, the Church. It is a very short book (only 117 verses in length), but one that you can read at many levels. Here the poet sings of the great power of true love. The many waters of trials and tests cannot put out the flame of love, earthly or divine. No material wealth can compare with it. Love is as strong as death. No wonder Martin Luther called the Song of Songs *das Hohelied*, the High Song. No wonder one of the ancient rabbis once said, "All the writings are holy, but the Song of Solomon is the Holy of Holies!" As a book, the Song of Solomon highlights more than any other that the Bible is a heavenly love story.

– 31 –

If my people, which are called by my name, shall humble themselves, and pray, and seek my face, and turn from their wicked ways; then will I hear from heaven, and will forgive their sin, and will heal their land.

2 Chronicles 7:14 (KJV)

If my people, who are called by my name, will humble themselves and pray and seek my face and turn from their wicked ways, then will I hear from heaven and will forgive their sin and will heal their land.

2 Chronicles 7:14 (NIV)

Solomon calls the people of Israel to start work on the Temple in Jerusalem, and from 2 Chronicles chapter 2 to chapter 4 the Temple is built. In the two chapters prior to 2 Chronicles 7:14, Solomon consecrates the magnificent Temple that the people have built. At the end of 2 Chronicles 6, Solomon prays that the Lord will come and make His resting place in this architectural wonder. In 2 Chronicles 7, the cloud of the glory of God fills the Temple and all the priests are overwhelmed. All start singing, "His love endures forever." Not long after, God appears to Solomon in a dream and tells him what to do whenever the Father's blessing lifts from Israel. He says that His children must humble themselves, pray, seek His face, and turn from wickedness. If they do that, His blessing will be restored; their sins will be forgiven, and the land will be healed. This verse has been the inspiration for millions who long for the Father to come and visit His people in power. It is the prayer that we must pray when we long for a fresh and mighty visitation of the Father's love in our own generation.

— 32 —

And the Lord was angry with Solomon, because his heart was turned from the Lord God of Israel, which had appeared unto him twice.

1 Kings 11:9 (KJV)

The Lord became angry with Solomon because his heart had turned away from the Lord, the God of Israel, who had appeared to him twice.

1 Kings 11:9 (NIV)

This is a critical verse in the unfolding drama of the Old Testament. Solomon has disobeyed God. He has coveted and accumulated horses, wives, and gold—the very things that God commanded the kings not to do in Deuteronomy 17:16–17. Solomon has fallen for the three main idols of power, sex, and money. He has replaced the love of the Father with the love of the world. He should not have pursued these toxic attachments, especially because God had appeared twice to him—once before he had dedicated the Temple (1 Kings 3:5) and once after (1 Kings 9:2). But Solomon sins, and the divine punishment for this is that there will be a division of his kingdom. This is exactly what happens. When Solomon dies and his son Rehoboam succeeds him, the kingdom is torn in two. The southern part (called Judah) remains centered on Jerusalem. The northern part (called Israel) is formed when ten of the twelve tribes refuse to submit to the rule of the king of Judah. We should always remember this: the Father longs for unity while the devil always works busily for division. When we sin, there is always a separation.

Division of the Two Kingdoms[3]

- 33 -

*And he said, I have been very jealous
for the Lord God of hosts: because
the children of Israel have forsaken thy
covenant, thrown down thine altars,
and slain thy prophets with the sword;
and I, even I only, am left; and they
seek my life, to take it away.*

1 Kings 19:14 (KJV)

*He replied, "I have been very zealous
for the Lord God Almighty. The Israelites have rejected your covenant,
broken down your altars, and put your
prophets to death with the sword. I am
the only one left, and now they are trying to kill me too."*

1 Kings 19:14 (NIV)

From the year 922 BC to 722 BC the north-ern kingdom is ruled by nineteen kings. During the reign of one of these, called Ahab (869–850 BC), Elijah the prophet is raised up by God. Elijah's name means "My God is Yah-weh." Ahab was a sinful king who had married Jezebel, a priestess of the pagan god Baal. Ahab allowed his wife to create a large entou-rage of pagan priests and prophets devoted to Baal—a god associated with sexual immo-rality. It is into this dire situation that Elijah is called to pronounce the Father's warnings and judgments. First Kings 19:14 comes shortly after Elijah's successful challenge to the 450 prophets of Baal on Mount Carmel. Elijah is on the run from the wicked queen Jezebel and hiding in a cave for the night. There he tells the Lord how he has been standing alone against the tide of darkness in the nation because he is jealous for the Lord's name. We have seen already that the Father is jealous for us. We need to become equally jealous for Him—jealous for His reputation as our loving, kind, holy Father.

— 34 —

Now there cried a certain woman of the wives of the sons of the prophets unto Elisha, saying, Thy servant my husband is dead; and thou knowest that thy servant did fear the Lord: and the creditor is come to take unto him my two sons to be bondmen.

2 Kings 4:1 (KJV)

The wife of a man from the company of the prophets cried out to Elisha, "Your servant my husband is dead, and you know that he revered the Lord. But now his creditor is coming to take my two boys as his slaves."

2 Kings 4:1 (NIV)

Elisha the prophet was Elijah's successor. Elisha's name means "My God is Salvation."

At the end of his ministry, Elijah is taken up to heaven in a chariot of fire (see 2 Kings 2:11–12). Having grieved his mentor's departure, Elisha takes hold of the prophetic mantle given to him by Elijah and begins his ministry in the northern kingdom. For sixty years he holds the office of prophet in Israel (892–832 BC). Elisha is given a double blessing by Elijah, so we find twice the number of miracles in Elisha's ministry as in his predecessor's. In 2 Kings 4, Elisha performs a miracle of provision for a widow. Her two sons have become orphans. They are now fatherless; they are also in danger of being sold into slavery. Elisha supernaturally supplies a superabundance of oil for the widow and her sons, so she can pay her debts and live on what remains. Elisha's conduct reveals how closely he embodies the Father's compassion for the widow and the orphan. Our heavenly Father will go to any lengths to prevent His sons and daughters becoming slaves.

– 35 –

When Israel was a child, then I loved
him, and called my son out of Egypt.

Hosea 11:1 (KJV)

When Israel was a child, I loved him,
and out of Egypt I called my son.

Hosea 11:1 (NIV)

The northern kingdom (Israel) falls to the Assyrian army in 722 BC. Samaria, its capital city, is destroyed. In the sixty years before Israel's fall, three prophets emerge in Israel to prophesy to the people about the impending destruction that their sins have brought upon themselves. Their names are Jonah, Amos, and Hosea. These three men form part of the "minor prophets" in the Old Testament. Hosea's name means "Salvation is of the Lord." He married an unfaithful prostitute called Gomer in order to highlight the unfaithfulness of Israel to her God. The Book of Hosea is a harsh warning to Israel to stop following foreign gods and to remain faithful to Yahweh. In this poignant verse God speaks as a father, reminding His people that He adopted Israel as His son and led her out of slavery. But now Israel is deciding to forsake her sonship and choose slavery instead. This will have terminal consequences for the northern kingdom. When we disobey our Father by worshiping other gods and idols, we stop behaving like sons and we start to live like slaves. When this happens, we need a fresh revelation of the Father's unrelenting kindness, which alone can lure us out of our addictions and transport us back to the Father's arms.

Minor Prophets

Group	Book	Approximate Dates
Prophets of Israel before the Assyrians conquered Israel	Jonah (preached to Nineveh)	790 BC
	Amos	752 BC
	Hosea	755-725 BC
Prophets of Judah before the Babylonians conquered Judah.	Obadiah	845 BC
	Joel	750 BC
	Micah	735-700 BC
	Nahum	626 BC
	Habakkuk	625-615 BC
	Zephaniah	625 BC
Prophets in Judah after the return of the Jews from exile in Babylon.	Haggai	520 BC
	Zechariah	520-518 BC
	Malachi	440 BC

— 36 —

*Therefore the Lord himself shall give
you a sign; Behold, a virgin shall conceive, and bear a son, and shall call his
name Immanuel.*

Isaiah 7:14 (KJV)

*Therefore the Lord himself will give
you a sign: The virgin will be with child
and will give birth to a son, and will call
him Immanuel.*

Isaiah 7:14 (NIV)

While the northern kingdom falls to the
Assyrians in 722 BC, the southern kingdom
of Judah continues until 586 BC, when it falls
to the Babylonians. A number of prophets
are called by God to speak to the people of
Judah over the centuries between 722 and
586 BC. One of the greatest of these prophets

is Isaiah, who prophesied six centuries before Jesus was born. His message is one of warning as well as hope. Isaiah 7:14 has long been regarded by Christians as one such prophecy of hope. Here Isaiah prophesies to the house of David, saying that a virgin will conceive and have a son whose name will be "Immanuel," which means "God with us." The word "virgin" is *almah* in Hebrew, meaning "a young unmarried woman." In the culture of the time, such a woman would certainly be a virgin, so the KJV and NIV are right to translate it "virgin." Many centuries later this prophecy will be applied to the Virgin Mary, mother of Jesus (see Matt. 1:23). Out of her womb, and out of her obedience, a Savior will be born from the house of David. This message, repeated every Christmas, is the world's only hope. It is a message from the very heart of the Father of Love.

– 37 –

For unto us a child is born, unto us a son is given: and the government shall be upon his shoulder: and his name shall be called Wonderful, Counsellor, The mighty God, The everlasting Father, The Prince of Peace.

Isaiah 9:6 (KJV)

For to us a child is born, to us a son is given, and the government will be on his shoulders. And he will be called Wonderful Counselor, Mighty God, Everlasting Father, Prince of Peace.

Isaiah 9:6 (NIV)

About 600 years before Jesus was born, Isaiah the prophet declared that a male child would be born. This son would reign on King David's throne and his rule would be everlasting. King David's reign lasted from about 1050 to 1010 BC, and during that time the Lord had made a covenant with David that his throne would be everlasting. Christians believe that this prophecy is ultimately fulfilled in Jesus of Nazareth. Jesus reigns forever. His kingdom (the kingdom of heaven) is eternal. Moreover, Jesus deserves all the names that Isaiah attributes to this unique, future, royal son: Wonderful, Counselor, Mighty God, Everlasting Father, Prince of Peace. Notice the title "Everlasting Father"—Jesus said, "Anyone who has seen me has seen the Father" (John 14:9). Jesus would come as the Son of the Everlasting Father who reveals what the Father is truly like. As the eternal Son, He alone would truly reveal the Everlasting Father. Thank God for Jesus! Without His birth on the earth, we would never have known that the God who created the universe is the Dad who loves us forever!

— 38 —

*But he was wounded for our transgres-
sions, he was bruised for our iniquities:
the chastisement of our peace was
upon him; and with his stripes we are
healed.*

Isaiah 53:5 (KJV)

*He was pierced for our transgressions,
he was crushed for our iniquities; the
punishment that brought us peace was
upon him, and by his wounds we are
healed.*

Isaiah 53:5 (NIV)

For Christians, the most important of all
Isaiah's prophecies is in Isaiah 53. Here Isaiah
has a vision of a Suffering Servant of Yahweh.
He sees that this man will grow up like any
ordinary, unremarkable mortal, that He will

be despised and rejected and become a man familiar with human suffering. He will be considered afflicted by God as He carries our sorrows and is wounded for our transgressions. But it will also be seen that the penalty He bore in our place would give us peace, and the pain that He suffered would bring us healing. Christians believe that all this points to the birth, life, and death of Jesus of Nazareth. Jesus lived a hidden life in Nazareth for many years. He looked like an ordinary Jewish man. There was nothing remarkable about His looks. This all led to Calvary where He became familiar with our suffering, acquainted with our grief. On the Cross, Jesus took our punishment; He made the supreme sacrifice, so that we might be reconciled to our Father in heaven. The whole of the Old Testament leads toward this great act of self-forgetful love. The turning point in the Father's love story is like the turning point in so many great stories—it is an act of sacrificial love. Isaiah saw it. We need to see it too.

— 39 —

But now, O Lord, thou art our father;
we are the clay, and thou our potter;
and we all are the work of thy hand.

Isaiah 64:8 (KJV)

O Lord, you are our Father. We are the
clay, you are the potter; we are all the
work of your hand.

Isaiah 64:8 (NIV)

Sometimes it is said that the revelation of God as Father comes only in the New Testament. This is an exaggeration. In Isaiah 64 the prophet reflects on how the people of the southern kingdom have departed from God's ways. He considers how God in the past has acted on their behalf, but now Judah is far from God because of the unrighteousness of the people. Yet God is the one who forms and fathers His people. He formed His people as a potter forms a lump of clay. He fathers His people as a loving father does. So, even while Judah's cities are laid waste and the Temple is in ruins, Isaiah can say, "But you are our Father, though Abraham does not know us or Israel acknowledge us; you, O LORD, are our Father, our Redeemer from of old is your name" (Isa. 63:16). Isaiah exalts God as loving Father as well as the Divine Potter. When we fall through our own sin, or when we are fractured by life, He takes all the broken pieces and glues them together with the golden lacquer of His glorious love, making the end product even more precious than it was before. What a great Dad this is! In His tender hands, all our ugly imperfections are beautified by His amazing and artistic kindness. There is no father like our Father!

– 40 –

But thou, Bethlehem Ephratah, though thou be little among the thousands of Judah, yet out of thee shall he come forth unto me that is to be ruler in Israel; whose goings forth have been from of old, from everlasting.

Micah 5:2 (KJV)

But you, Bethlehem Ephrathah, though you are small among the clans of Judah, out of you will come for me one who will be ruler over Israel, whose origins are from of old, from ancient times.

Micah 5:2 (NIV)

Micah prophesies in Judah during the reign of King Hezekiah (see Jer. 26:18). Micah lived at a time of instability in his region. The

Assyrian army had conquered the northern kingdom, and the rich were exploiting the poor in the southern kingdom, where Micah lived. Micah was appalled by the people's disobedience to God's covenant and spoke out against the injustices of his day. In Micah 5:2 he prophesies that a ruler in Israel will come from the tiny town of Bethlehem (meaning "house of bread") Ephrathah (meaning "fertile"). Micah narrows the birthplace of the Messiah to the town where David was born and crowned. In Matthew 2:1–6 we see this prophecy fulfilled in the birth of Jesus. The Jewish Talmud (a record of the teaching of the rabbis, second century BC) also spoke of this: "The King Messiah…from where does he come forth? From the royal city of Bethlehem in Judah." Micah prophesies the birthplace of Jesus the Messiah. What a revelation of the Father's love there is in this prophecy. Our Father takes hold of tiny, insignificant places and turns them into epicenters of heavenly visitation. He is always busy doing this, not just with places, but with people. People like

you and me! Take heart. He has a grand purpose for your life.

— 41 —

*The Lord thy God in the midst of thee
is mighty; he will save, he will rejoice
over thee with joy; he will rest in his
love, he will joy over thee with singing.*

                              Zephaniah 3:17 (KJV)

*The Lord your God is with you, he
is mighty to save. He will take great
delight in you, he will quiet you with
his love, he will rejoice over you with
singing.*

                              Zephaniah 3:17 (NIV)

Zephaniah is a "minor prophet" who
prophesied in the southern kingdom during

the reign of Josiah in the seventh century BC. His name means "He whom the Lord has hidden." The two kings prior to Josiah had brought idolatry into Judah and Jerusalem, especially the worship of Baal. Zephaniah's book is only three chapters and the overriding theme is one of impending judgment—judgment for Judah and Jerusalem for their sins (chapter 1), judgment for the nations of the world (chapter 2). In chapter 3 (verses 1–8) Zephaniah rounds on the ruling classes and the priests in Jerusalem, giving them dire warnings, before turning to the long-term future and the coming of the kingdom of God in the future (verses 9–20). On the day of the coming of God's kingdom, God's presence will be felt and His delight over Jerusalem will be known. He will refresh His people with His love and will spin around and sing for joy over them, like a deliriously happy Father. While this prophecy was originally for Jerusalem, it is one we too can activate and enjoy. When we too return to the Father in repentance, we too can hear Him rejoicing over us with singing. We too can rest in His quietening love. We too can enjoy the revelation of His great delight in us. There truly is no party like the Father's party!

– 42 –

For I know the thoughts that I think toward you, saith the Lord, thoughts of peace, and not of evil, to give you an expected end.

Jeremiah 29:11 (KJV)

"I know the plans I have for you," declares the Lord, "plans to prosper you and not to harm you, plans to give you hope and a future."

Jeremiah 29:11 (NIV)

Jeremiah is known as one of the "major prophets." He was called by God to confront the people of Judah concerning their worship of idols (625–575 BC). In this and in many other ways they had broken the covenant. God therefore declares that they are going to experience the consequences of their own orphan-hearted rebellion—namely, destruction. The disaster of the Babylonian siege of Jerusalem had not yet happened, so the people didn't take kindly to Jeremiah's words of warning. He was attacked and imprisoned by his own people, but when King Nebuchadnezzar sacked Jerusalem he released Jeremiah from prison and treated him well. Although Jeremiah is known as "the weeping prophet"—not surprisingly, given how his own people mistreated him—his prophecy here in Jeremiah 29:11 is one full of hope. He declares that after 70 years Babylon's rule will be ended, and the Jewish remnant will return from exile to the land. God knows the plans He has for His people and they are for a hope and a future. Whenever we face hardship, there is always something to hope for; our Father loves us too much to allow us

to languish in despair. He wants our hearts to
overflow with hope.

– 43 –

*But this shall be the covenant that I will
make with the house of Israel; After
those days, saith the Lord, I will put my
law in their inward parts, and write it in
their hearts; and will be their God, and
they shall be my people.*

Jeremiah 31:33 (KJV)

*"This is the covenant I will make with
the house of Israel after that time,"
declares the Lord. "I will put my law in
their minds and write it on their hearts.
I will be their God, and they will be my
people."*

Jeremiah 31:33 (NIV)

Jeremiah prophesies that there are days coming when the Lord will bring the remnant of Judah and Israel back from exile to the land of their forefathers. God promises to restore the fortunes of the land to what they were before the exile. God promises that a righteous branch will sprout from David's line—a promise of the birth of Jesus the Messiah. He declares that He has loved His people with an everlasting love. The Temple will be restored, and countless people will make pilgrimage there with shouts of joy, all because Israel is the Father's dear son (see Jer. 31:20). In those days Jeremiah prophesies that the Lord will form a new covenant with His people. This time the law will no longer be something external, such as writing on stone. It will be an internal reality as the Spirit of God writes it on their hearts. Six hundred years later this was to be fulfilled when the Spirit of God was poured out on the Day of Pentecost, and it is still being fulfilled today! From that day on, God's children no longer have God's words written on tablets of stone. They are emblazoned instead on the parchment of our hearts, written in the fiery letters of the Holy Spirit.

– 44 –

Now it came to pass in the thirtieth year, in the fourth month, in the fifth day of the month, as I was among the captives by the river of Chebar, that the heavens were opened, and I saw visions of God.

Ezekiel 1:1 (KJV)

In the thirtieth year, in the fourth month on the fifth day, while I was among the exiles by the Kebar River, the heavens were opened and I saw visions of God.

Ezekiel 1:1 (NIV)

Eventually the southern kingdom (Judah) follows the same path to destruction as that taken by Israel. As the sixth century BC begins, Babylon is the world's superpower. Led by Nebuchadnezzar, the Babylonian army sacks Jerusalem, destroys the Temple, and takes the priceless treasures of the Temple, including the Ark of the Covenant, back to Babylon. The remnant of people in Judah—about 50,000 people—is taken as captives into exile in 586 BC. Babylon rules the Promised Land—the land that the people of Judah have left—until 539 BC. In the sixty years or so from 600 to 539 BC, prophets such as Ezekiel are raised up by God to speak to the Jewish people. Ezekiel's name means "God will strengthen," a fitting one for his message. Ezekiel received many fortifying visions while he was in Babylon—such as the dry bones coming to life (Ezekiel 37) and the restored Temple as the source of a life-giving river (Ezekiel 47). Here in the first verse of his book, Ezekiel describes how in Babylon the heavens were opened and he had visions of God. Everyone, sooner or later, needs a vision of God. Jesus gives us the most profound picture of all—of God as the most loving and perfect Father, a Father who comes to the aid of His children when they experience the tragic fallout from their rebellion.

– 45 –

A new heart also will I give you, and a new spirit will I put within you: and I will take away the stony heart out of your flesh, and I will give you an heart of flesh.

Ezekiel 36:26 (KJV)

I will give you a new heart and put a new spirit in you; I will remove from you your heart of stone and give you a heart of flesh.

Ezekiel 36:26 (NIV)

One of Ezekiel's most important prophecies of hope concerns a future time when God will put a new spirit within the hearts of His people. Many of the people of Judah were now in exile in Babylon (modern Iraq). This was because they had engaged in idolatrous practices and had broken God's covenant. But Ezekiel brings good news. There's a day coming when the Lord will restore the land to them, and Israel and Judah will be reunited as one nation back home, under the leadership of one king. There will then be a spiritual renewal in which God will sprinkle clean water on them, and He will give them a new heart and a new spirit (see Ezek. 36:24–29). In verse 27 He says that He will put His Spirit in people's hearts so that they will *want* to obey His laws. The gift of the indwelling Spirit will be given as Jesus establishes the new covenant through His death on the Cross. This gift of the Holy Spirit is one of the Father's greatest presents to His children. The Holy Spirit gives us the grace and the love to become soft-hearted rather than hard-hearted in our relationship with the Father. Through the Holy Spirit, we are given new hearts—hearts that obey the Father out of love not law.

— 46 —

The king answered unto Daniel, and said, Of a truth it is, that your God is a God of gods, and a Lord of kings, and a revealer of secrets, seeing thou couldest reveal this secret.

Daniel 2:47 (KJV)

The king said to Daniel, "Surely your God is the God of gods and the Lord

of kings and a revealer of mysteries, for
you were able to reveal this mystery."

Daniel 2:47 (NIV)

Daniel is in captivity in Babylon along with the survivors ("the remnant") of the people of Judah. Daniel chapter 2 describes a test given to Daniel. King Nebuchadnezzar has a dream that troubles him. He calls his court astrologers to interpret it for him. However, he does not tell them the dream. They fail in the task, so Daniel prays. God tells him the dream and its interpretation. The dream is of the destruction of a statue with a head of gold, chest and arms of silver, belly and thighs of iron, feet of iron and clay. Daniel tells the king that this refers to his kingdom (the gold head) and four others that will follow, all of which will come to an end. But there will be a kingdom that will last forever (the kingdom of God). Daniel passes his test (and all the others described in this book) and the pagan king declares that Daniel's God is the God of gods, the Lord of kings, and the Revealer of Mysteries. This is a reminder to all of us how faithful our heavenly Father is to us when we are faithful to Him, especially when we are under pressure from a godless culture.

– 47 –

Then he answered and spake unto me, saying, This is the word of the Lord unto Zerubbabel, saying, Not by might, nor by power, but by my spirit, saith the Lord of hosts.

Zechariah 4:6 (KJV)

So he said to me, "This is the word of the Lord to Zerubbabel: 'Not by might nor by power, but by my Spirit,' says the Lord Almighty."

Zechariah 4:6 (NIV)

In 538 BC, the Babylonians had been replaced by the Persians as the world's superpower. This brought the Persian King Cyrus to power. He released the Jewish remnant from their captivity in exile. Led by Zerubbabel and Joshua, 50,000 Jews returned from Babylon to the land and for two years worked on rebuilding the Temple. Then in 536 BC the work ground to a halt. For over fifteen years the two leaders were discouraged at the inactivity of God's people, until two prophets—Zechariah and Haggai—came and spoke words of encouragement. Here Zechariah tells Zerubbabel that the new Temple will be built but that this will be achieved not by human power but by the Spirit of God. Thereafter God's Spirit stirred the people to work and the Second Temple was completed in 516 BC. All this highlights the believer's absolute dependence on the Holy Spirit in building anything for the Lord of Hosts (literally, "the Lord of the Armies of Heaven"). The true children of God lean on the Father and depend on Him entirely. Filled with the Holy Spirit, rather than relying on their own human resources, they can achieve truly great results.

– 48 –

Then he said unto them, Go your way, eat the fat, and drink the sweet, and send portions unto them for whom nothing is prepared: for this day is holy unto our Lord: neither be ye sorry; for the joy of the Lord is your strength.

Nehemiah 8:10 (KJV)

Nehemiah said, "Go and enjoy choice food and sweet drinks, and send some to those who have nothing prepared. This day is sacred to our Lord. Do not grieve, for the joy of the Lord is your strength."

Nehemiah 8:10 (NIV)

After Zerubbabel and Joshua had completed the rebuilding of the Temple in 516 BC, it was time for the city of Jerusalem to be restored as well. In 459 BC Ezra, a Jewish priest still in Babylon, led about 10,000 of his expatriates back to the land. He brought the Jewish people back to the law and challenged them to be a holy nation at a time when there were intermarriages taking place with other nations. Ezra reappears in Nehemiah chapter 8 when the city walls have been rebuilt by Nehemiah. The Book of the Law is brought out, and Ezra and the Levites read it night and day and explain its meaning to the people. All the people begin to weep because they are so powerfully moved by the words of God's Book. But Nehemiah (the governor) and Ezra (the priest) tell them to stop weeping and to start rejoicing. The joy of the Lord is their strength. It is a hallmark of God's people. So now it's time to celebrate! The sons and daughters of God know that the Father's joy is their strength.

– 49 –

And it shall come to pass afterward, that I will pour out my spirit upon all flesh; and your sons and your daughters shall prophesy, your old men shall dream dreams, your young men shall see visions.

Joel 2:28 (KJV)

And afterward, I will pour out my Spirit on all people. Your sons and daughters will prophesy, your old men will dream dreams, your young men will see visions.

Joel 2:28 (NIV)

Joel's name means "Yahweh is God." Very little is known about who he was or when he prophesied. Some argue that he prophesied in the eighth century BC. Others propose that he prophesied after the exile, in the fifth century BC. Joel 2:28 is perhaps the most famous of his prophecies. Like other Old Testament prophets, Joel prophesies a day when God will pour out His Spirit (see also Isa. 32:15; 44:1–5; and Ezek. 39:29). Joel 2:28 forms part of a promise that Yahweh will bless His people with His visible, glorious presence and never again allow them to be put to shame. The fulfilment of this will be in Jerusalem hundreds of years later, when the Holy Spirit falls upon the 120 disciples of Jesus on the Day of Pentecost (see Acts 2:1–21). Then the long drought of the Holy Spirit, lasting 400 years, will come to an end with a deluge of the Father's love from heaven. This is a constant reminder to all those who claim to know the Father that we must be people constantly filled with the Holy Spirit, not relying on our own wisdom and strength.

*And he shall turn the heart of the
fathers to the children, and the heart of
the children to their fathers, lest I come
and smite the earth with a curse.*

Malachi 4:6 (KJV)

*He will turn the hearts of the fathers
to their children, and the hearts of the
children to their fathers; or else I will
come and strike the land with a curse.*

Malachi 4:6 (NIV)

With these words of the fifth-century
prophet Malachi, the Old Testament closes.
The story of the Old Testament began, as
we've seen, with the creation of the world
and the fall of humankind. In the Garden of
Eden, the adversary of God tempted Eve
and Adam and they fell from their position

as a daughter and son into the orphan state. Thereafter the Father adopted a people—Israel—as His cherished firstborn son. From Abraham onward, the people of Israel have been the focus of the Father's covenant love. However, Israel falls time and time again for the adversary's temptations. Throughout the Old Testament he works behind the scenes to pull God's people again and again into the orphan state. But the Old Testament ends with a great prospect, a time when there will be reconciliation between children and their earthly fathers, and, by implication, between human beings and the Perfect Father. It will be with the coming of Jesus—God's One and Only Son—that this promise is fulfilled. Only then will the hearts of human beings be turned toward the heart of the Father, and the heart of the Father turned toward their hearts too.

THE NEW TESTAMENT

New Testament Timeline

40	BC	Herod the Great made King of Judea by Marc Antony
27	BC	Founding of the Roman Empire
20	BC	Herod the Great starts Temple rebuilding program
6	BC	Jesus' birth
4	BC	King Herod the Great dies
26-36	AD	Pontius Pilate is governor of Judea
26-28	AD	John the Baptist's ministry
27-30	AD	Jesus' ministry
30	AD	Crucifixion and resurection of Jesus
31	AD	Stephen martyred (Acts 6-8)
34-35	AD	Conversion of Saul (who becomes Paul, Acts 9)
38	AD	Peter baptizes the first Gentiles (Acts 10)
44-46	AD	Paul's first missionary journey
47	AD	First recorded use of the word "Christian" in Antioch
48-49	AD	Council at Jerusalem (Acts 15)
49-52	AD	Paul's second missionary journey
53-57	AD	Paul's third missionary journey
58-68	AD	Paul's final missionary journey and martyrdom in Rome
70	AD	Destruction of the Temple in Jerusalem

– 51 –

For unto you is born this day in the city of David a Saviour, which is Christ the Lord.

Luke 2:11 (KJV)

Today in the town of David a Savior has been born to you; he is Christ the Lord.

Luke 2:11 (NIV)

The entire course of history is changed in the sound of a baby crying in a humble dwelling in Bethlehem. This is where the Father's love story begins to turn in a redemptive direction. Micah the prophet had declared that this town would be the birthplace of a ruler in Israel, and this decree was regarded by the earliest Christians as a messianic prophecy (a prediction concerning the coming Messiah). Luke, who engaged in a meticulous process of historical research, discovered that a group of shepherds out on the hills had been visited by angels. This is a surprise because the shepherd's profession was a poor and despised one in that culture. Not so in heaven. It's the humble, marginalized, and grubby shepherds who get to hear the news first! The angels tell these shepherds that the one who has just been born in Bethlehem is none other than the Lord. In the world of the shepherds, only one human being was called "Lord" by the people of the day—the Roman emperor, and he ruled through force. But there is one now born in Bethlehem who is greater than Caesar, and who will rule the world with the power of love, not the love of power. This is the Father's Son—the One who has come to show us the way back to the Father's arms.

– 52 –

And the Word was made flesh, and dwelt among us, (and we beheld his glory, the glory as of the only begotten of the Father,) full of grace and truth.

John 1:14 (KJV)

The Word became flesh and made his dwelling among us. We have seen his glory, the glory of the One and Only, who came from the Father, full of grace and truth.

John 1:14 (NIV)

At the beginning of history, God spoke the universe and the earth into being. Through the power of His word, everything was created from nothing. At the beginning of John's Gospel, Jesus is called "the Word" (*Logos* in Greek, the language of the New Testament).

Jesus is the Word that was with the Father at the beginning of time. Jesus is the Word who is God from eternity to eternity. The one born as a baby in Bethlehem is therefore no ordinary mortal. He is not just the greatest of all prophets and teachers. He is the Word of the Father made flesh. He is God with skin on. He is the infinite become an infant. In Jesus, Yahweh has come to camp out among us. John (the writer of the Gospel), and those with him, lived and walked with Jesus-the-Word, and they saw God's glory in His human flesh. They knew that Jesus is the only Son by nature; that He is one of our kind, and that He is also one of a kind. Without Jesus, we would still be spiritual orphans, separated from the Father's love. But now, thanks to Jesus stepping down from heaven and entering the dust of the earth, we are orphans no more. We can become the adopted children of God!

And lo a voice from heaven, saying,
This is my beloved Son, in whom I am
well pleased.

Matthew 3:17 (KJV)

And a voice from heaven said, "This
is my Son, whom I love; with him I am
well pleased."

Matthew 3:17 (NIV)

Jesus grew from a child to a boy and from a boy to a man. There is little known about His childhood. There is a lot known about His adulthood. Aged about thirty, Jesus of Nazareth comes to the River Jordan and offers Himself for baptism by John the Baptist. John baptizes Jesus, and as Jesus comes up from the water the heavens are opened and the Father speaks words of affection over Jesus, telling Him that He is His Son, and that He is pleased with Him. This is an affirmation of Jesus' existing sonship, not an adoption into new sonship. Jesus was already the one and only Son of the Father. In the next statement, the Father reveals His unconditional acceptance of His Son. The Father's acceptance is based on the Son's position, not the Son's performance. God says, "I'm proud of You" even before Jesus has started His ministry! Before Jesus has preached a sermon, healed the sick, delivered the demonized, cleansed the lepers, or raised the dead, the Father says, "You're the pride of My life!" For those of us who have always had to earn approval from a father, this is a radical departure from the norm. What a loving Father this is, who applauds His Son before He's even started His ministry!

— 54 —

From that time Jesus began to preach, and to say, Repent: for the kingdom of heaven is at hand.

Matthew 4:17 (KJV)

From that time on Jesus began to preach, "Repent, for the kingdom of heaven is near."

Matthew 4:17 (NIV)

After Jesus has been baptized, He is tested by Satan for forty days and nights in the desert. There is a lesson here. Just because you have a revelation of the Father's love, that doesn't mean you're going to live a trouble-free life! Jesus goes straight from hearing His Dad in the river to facing the devil in the desert. Having successfully resisted, Jesus comes out of the wilderness and begins to preach the message of the kingdom of heaven. God already rules in heaven, but planet earth has been under Satan's rule since the temptation of Adam and Eve in the Garden of Eden. Now the reign of God is entering history. Heaven is invading earth through Jesus of Nazareth. The Son is bringing the Father's rule to earth and the adversary's reign is being directly confronted. Jesus tells His listeners that heaven's rule is very near to them and that they are to repent—they are to turn from self-rule (sin) to God's rule (the kingdom). In this kingdom, sins are forgiven, sicknesses are healed, poverty is eradicated, demons are expelled, and even the dead are raised. The kingdom of God is truly heaven on earth. It is the Father's life-transforming love and power made manifest in our midst. Don't you want to be a part of that?

Blessed are the meek: for they shall inherit the earth.

Matthew 5:5 (KJV)

Blessed are the meek, for they will inherit the earth.

Matthew 5:5 (NIV)

Jesus chooses twelve disciples or apprentices to follow Him. These twelve men remind us of the twelve tribes of Israel. Jesus is accordingly fulfilling the calling that the Father gave to Israel, to be a faithful son who brings the Father's blessing to the whole world. As part of His mission, in Matthew chapters 5–7 Jesus teaches His famous Sermon on the Mount. This is a sermon in which He describes the kind of lifestyle expected of someone who enters the kingdom of heaven. Jesus tells the disciples that they will be blessed if they behave as the Father wants. "Blessed are the meek," He says. Meekness is not weakness. It is great strength harnessed to God's will. It is the word used for the reining in of a wild horse. "Blessed are those who allow themselves to be reined in by the Lord. They will inherit the earth." When Jesus returns at the end of history, those who have been harnessed to the work of the kingdom will live forever and enjoy the full blessings of the new heavens and the new earth. The Father is looking for people like this—sons and daughters who have been through a process of training for reigning, a process in which all the unbridled energy that went into serving the self is now tamed and redirected into serving the purposes of God in our generation.

— 56 —

After this manner therefore pray ye:
Our Father which art in heaven, Hal-
lowed be thy name.

Matthew 6:9 (KJV)

This, then, is how you should pray:
"Our Father in heaven, hallowed be
your name."

Matthew 6:9 (NIV)

The Lord's Prayer, beginning "Our Father," is the most famous prayer in history. Jesus is teaching His twelve apprentices here about prayer. They have seen Him pray and they want to know how to do it too. Jesus tells them to begin by praying "Our Father." The word Jesus would have used is the Aramaic word *Abba*. Aramaic was the language Jesus spoke. *Abba* is an intimate word. It is the first word learned by a child in at least four Middle Eastern countries even to this day. It means something like "Daddy." Jesus taught His disciples to begin their prayers by addressing God in the most intimate, relational, and affectionate terms. He told them to call God "Papa"! He wanted them to hallow *Abba's* name, to hold it sacred. And He wanted them to remember that God is a *heavenly* Father. Unlike earthly fathers, He is infinite, not finite, and He is perfect, not imperfect. All this shows that Jesus came to reveal that God is *Abba*, Father, and that God is relational, not remote. When we pray, we open a conversation with the most adoring Dad. Prayer, at the end of the day, is communion with the perfect Father. We should speak to God as we speak to a really good dad.

*But seek ye first the kingdom of God,
and his righteousness; and all these
things shall be added unto you.*

Matthew 6:33 (KJV)

*Seek first his kingdom and his righ-
teousness, and all these things will be
given to you as well.*

Matthew 6:33 (NIV)

Jesus teaches His disciples that the greatest priority of their lives is to seek the kingdom of God. As children of the perfect Father,
their first passion must always be to hunger
and thirst for the reign and the righteousness
of God on earth. This must begin in their lives
first. The apprentices of Jesus must want to
see the Father's rule coming into history, and
they must begin by placing everything that

they are and do under God's rule. This means their character, their dreams, their relationships, their possessions must be submitted to the loving reign of God. They must allow the Father's righteousness to become their own. In other words, they must live in a right relationship with the Father, saying and doing the right things according to His norms. When they do that, everything will be provided by their Father—clothes, food, and everything else besides. All this shows that those who follow Jesus must live counter-culturally. They must not seek material, temporary things (like money) first. That is what the world does. They must put first things first and pursue spiritual, eternal realities (like love) before all other things.

— 58 —

If ye then, being evil, know how to give good gifts unto your children, how much more shall your Father which is in heaven give good things to them that ask him?

Matthew 7:11 (KJV)

If you, then, though you are evil, know how to give good gifts to your children, how much more will your Father in heaven give good gifts to those who ask him!

Matthew 7:11 (NIV)

How is a person to obey the teachings of Jesus? Jesus tells His apprentices that they are to live a life that is more righteous than that of the Pharisees, the ultra-orthodox and observant Jews of His day. He says that the disciples must be authentic, living on the inside what they profess to be on the outside. That's tough by any standard! How on earth does anyone achieve such a high calling of integrity and purity? Here's the answer. Jesus says that we have a Father who loves giving good gifts to His children. Even earthly fathers like doing this, and earthly fathers are imperfect. Unredeemed, earthly fathers are "evil" (or "sinful"). But our God is a perfect *Abba*, or Daddy, and if we ask Him trustingly like a child He will give us the good gift of the power of His Holy Spirit to help us fulfil our calling. We will become more and more like the Son as we resolve to take on the characteristics of our Father with the help of this Holy Spirit. Aren't you grateful that you don't have to go it alone? You have the Holy Spirit, your heavenly Father's gift, to help you.

– 59 –

Come unto me, all ye that labour and are heavy laden, and I will give you rest.

Matthew 11:28 (KJV)

*Come to me, all you who are weary
and burdened, and I will give you rest.*

Matthew 11:28 (NIV)

This great invitation follows Jesus' words in Matthew 11:27: "All things have been committed to me by my Father. No one knows the Son except the Father, and no one knows the Father except the Son and those to whom the Son chooses to reveal him." Jesus has been celebrating the fact that His apprentices are hearing truths that have been hidden from the wise and the sophisticated. The Father has chosen to reveal His secrets to little children, to the disciples. Now Jesus teaches that no one can get to know *Abba* Father unless the Son introduces them to Him. The Son reveals the Father. Once we have had a personal, direct revelation of the Father's love, all striving to earn God's approval comes to an end. The yoke becomes easy and the burden becomes light. Instead of resting from work, we work from rest. Revelation of the Father's love leads to a joyful spirituality of Sabbath rest. You can't learn to work from rest until you have encountered the Father's love. Once you have stood in the river with Jesus, once you have heard the Father's words of affirmation over you, you will never again work *for* approval; you will work *from* approval. What a difference the Father's love makes when it is a felt reality in our hearts!

— 60 —

Verily I say unto you, Except ye be converted, and become as little children, ye shall not enter into the kingdom of heaven.

Matthew 18:3 (KJV)

*I tell you the truth, unless you change
and become like little children, you will
never enter the kingdom of heaven.*

Matthew 18:3 (NIV)

Jesus came not to start a religion but to start a relationship—a relationship between us and the world's greatest Dad. Jesus came to reveal *Abba* Father's love and to die on the Cross so that we could be reconciled to our Father in heaven. Put like this, you can see that this is all about relationship. Jesus lived out of that deep, personal relationship with the Father. He wants us to as well. This is what Jesus is teaching His disciples here. He calls a little child to come and sit with Him. The disciples are asking who is the greatest in the kingdom of heaven. Jesus' answer is to point at the child and tell the disciples that they cannot even enter the kingdom unless they become childlike. Their egos must decrease. Their pride must be crucified. The disciples must allow the Father to transform them so that they become one of His "little ones." Like Alice, in *Alice in Wonderland*, they will never enter the enticing landscape of the kingdom unless they first become very small. Once they do, they will know the Father's love in their personal experience, and they will see the reign of the Father come in power and love wherever they set their feet.

— 61 —

It is easier for a camel to go through the eye of a needle, than for a rich man to enter into the kingdom of God.

Mark 10:25 (KJV)

It is easier for a camel to go through the eye of a needle than for a rich man to enter the kingdom of God.

Mark 10:25 (NIV)

A rich man has just come to Jesus in the presence of the disciples. The man has asked Jesus what he must do to inherit eternal life. We might translate that as, "What must I do to be sure of going to heaven when I die?" Jesus tells the man to sell all he has and give the money to the poor. The disciples are startled. How can a rich person enter the kingdom of God? Jesus then uses a striking word picture involving a camel passing through the eye of a needle. What did Jesus mean by that? Many solutions have been offered: that it refers to a camel passing through a narrow mountain pass, or through a small door fixed in a gate, or through the head of a tiny sewing needle. However, Jesus spoke in Aramaic, and the Aramaic word translated "camel" (*gamla*) can also be translated "rope." It may be that Jesus is saying that it is easier for a rope to go through the eye of a sewing needle than for a rich man to enter the kingdom of God. Whatever the right interpretation, Jesus is showing a very wealthy man that he first needs to empty himself of his love for the world—his love for money, sex, power—before he can experience the Father's love. There must be an emptying before there can be a filling, and that's true for all of us.

— 62 —

And Jesus answering said unto them, Render to Caesar the things that are Caesar's, and to God the things that are God's.

Mark 12:17 (KJV)

Give to Caesar what is Caesar's and to God what is God's.

Mark 12:17 (NIV)

In this episode, Jesus is being challenged by some opponents who are trying to catch Him out. They ask Him if they should pay taxes to Caesar. If He says yes, then He will be seen to be supporting the hated Roman occupiers. If He says no, then He will be seen to be committing treason. Jesus asks for a denarius, a coin. He asks whose image it bears. They reply, "Caesar's." He then utters this saying about giving to Caesar what belongs to Caesar and giving to God what belongs to God. Jesus seems to be saying that it is right to pay taxes to the government of the day and it is also right to give to God. But there is more to it than this. There was an image of Caesar on the coin. The coin would therefore have been made "in the image of Caesar." Jesus knows that as human beings we are all made "in the image of God," who is far greater than Caesar. The money Caesar asks for is therefore nothing compared to what God asks for. God asks for everything from us because we are made in His image! If we truly want to become sons and daughters of God, if we truly want to become heroes in the Father's love story on earth, then we must become like our heavenly Father in everything we think, say, and do. We must be like coins imprinted with the Father's smile.

— 63 —

And he arose, and came to his father. But when he was yet a great way off, his father saw him, and had compassion, and ran, and fell on his neck, and kissed him.

Luke 15:20 (KJV)

So he got up and went to his father. But while he was still a long way off, his father saw him and was filled with compassion for him; he ran to his son, threw his arms around him and kissed him.

Luke 15:20 (NIV)

Jesus is being confronted by teachers of the law who are criticizing Him for having meals with sinners. Jesus responds to His critics by telling three stories in Luke 15. The third one concerns a son who demands his inheritance from his father. In the Middle East, to ask for your inheritance while your father is still alive is effectively to say, "I wish you were dead." It is the most shameful insult. The father, though, is magnificent. He lets the boy have what he wants so that he can in time discover what he really needs. The son duly leaves with the cash and the dad waits day and night for his boy to return. One day, this exceptional father sees his boy returning, emaciated and ruined. He is filled with compassion and he lifts his robe to run like the wind to greet him. He throws his arms around his wretched child's neck and kisses him repeatedly. What a picture! What a father! Jesus uses this story to tell His critics what God is really like. He is not the God that they have been portraying, who puts heavy legalistic burdens around peoples' necks. He is the world's most amazing Father, like the father in Luke 15. He is the God of embrace, not exclusion. And He loves throwing parties for returning sons and daughters. Like Jesus, He loves having meals with sinners.

— 64 —

Jesus answered and said unto him, Verily, verily, I say unto thee, Except a man be born again, he cannot see the kingdom of God.

John 3:3 (KJV)

Jesus declared, "I tell you the truth, no one can see the kingdom of God unless he is born again."

John 3:3 (NIV)

Early on in His public ministry, Jesus is visited by a member of the ruling council of the Pharisees called Nicodemus. Nicodemus comes to Jesus by night, no doubt because he does not want to be seen visiting this radical *hasid*, or holy man. Nicodemus acknowledges that Jesus of Nazareth is a man who has come from God because of the miracles that He has been performing. Jesus answers by telling Nicodemus that a person cannot see the kingdom of God unless they are born again. The kingdom of God and the Fatherhood of God are the two central themes of Jesus' teaching. God's kingdom refers to His reign on earth, evidenced by the miracles that Nicodemus has referenced. Rebirth is the portal into this kingdom. Jesus tells Nicodemus that he must be spiritually reborn if he is to witness the reality of the reign of heaven on earth. He must have a radical new start in which he becomes a true child of God—one marked by relationship, not religion. Put another way, he must receive a revelation of the Fatherhood of God before he can ever see a manifestation of the kingdom of God. By the end of John's gospel, Nicodemus will be bringing burial spices to venerate the dead Jesus. Something has clearly changed in his heart. And that's where true change always starts.

— 65 —

For God so loved the world, that he gave his only begotten Son, that whosoever believeth in him should not perish, but have everlasting life.

John 3:16 (KJV)

For God so loved the world that he gave his one and only Son, that whoever believes in him shall not perish but have eternal life.

John 3:16 (NIV)

In this magnificent verse from the Gospel of John we are given an insight into the reason why God sent Jesus to the earth two thousand or so years ago. First, we learn that

God so *loved* the world. The Father couldn't stand to see humanity living in the orphan state any longer. This is because He loved the world—loved it with a sacrificial, affectionate, everlasting love. So, second, He gave His *one and only* Son. The language here is reminiscent of the story of Abraham in Genesis 22. There Abraham was prepared to sacrifice his son Isaac out of obedience to God. Isaac is described as *yahid* in the Hebrew language, as Abraham's "one and only, precious one." Our heavenly Father was prepared to give His precious one too. Third, the Father gave what was dearest to Him in order to save human beings from eternal separation from His love, from "perishing." That is some mission statement! What we need to do by way of response is to believe in Jesus and enter an eternal friendship with Him. That way we get to enjoy the Father's embrace—an embrace in which we experience our own spiritual homecoming, as we leave the orphan state behind and enter a relationship of oneness with the

Father, through Jesus, and with the help of the Holy Spirit.

– 66 –

And Jesus said unto them, I am the
bread of life: he that cometh to me
shall never hunger; and he that belie-
veth on me shall never thirst.

John 6:35 (KJV)

Then Jesus declared, "I am the bread
of life. He who comes to me will never
go hungry, and he who believes in me
will never be thirsty."

John 6:35 (NIV)

Jesus has performed a great miracle at the start of John chapter 6; He has multiplied five loaves into enough bread to feed 5,000 men (more like 15,000 people if you include the women and children as well). This startles the crowd who follow Jesus across the Lake of Galilee in order to catch up with Him. They engage in discussion with Jesus. Continuing the theme of bread, they announce that Moses gave *manna* (supernatural bread) to their forefathers in the wilderness after the Exodus from Egypt. Jesus tells them it wasn't Moses who gave them this bread from heaven. It was their heavenly Father. The crowd then say, "Give us this bread." Jesus replies, "I am the Bread." Notice the phrase, "I am." God revealed Himself to Moses as "I am who I am." Jesus is using the divine name in relation to Himself here. He is telling His listeners that He is divine. He is also telling them that He alone can satisfy the spiritual hunger that they and all human beings have. The Father's love is profoundly attracted to our spiritual hunger. The more self-satisfied we are, the less likely we are to experience it. We must become empty before we can be filled. When we become empty and desperate, we discover that our Father is a miraculous baker,

and that He makes fresh bread for all who are
hungry.

— 67 —

*The thief cometh not, but for to steal,
and to kill, and to destroy: I am come
that they might have life, and that they
might have it more abundantly.*

John 10:10 (KJV)

*The thief comes only to steal and kill
and destroy; I have come that they
may have life, and have it to the full.*

John 10:10 (NIV)

There are two words for life in the Greek
language in which John's Gospel was originally written. There is first the word *bios*, from
which we get the word "biology." This means
finite, physical life. Then there is the word *zoe*,

from which we get the word "zoology." This means infinite, spiritual life. In this famous saying Jesus announces that He has come to earth in order to give those who follow Him a life that lasts forever, an abundant life that satisfies the deepest longings of the human soul, a life that no worldly, material comforts can deliver. This is far more than just biological existence; it is heavenly vitality. The problem here is that the devil does the exact opposite. He steals everything that gives a person life. He has been doing that since the Garden of Eden, where he robbed our first parents of the life that the Father had given them. The good news is that Jesus is far stronger and has come to defeat the adversary and to restore to us what the enemy has stolen. If we want to experience the super-abundant life of our perfect Father, we must believe in Jesus and renounce the devil, and we must continue doing this every day. There is truly a battle on, but our Father in heaven is the life-giver. Lean on Him and He will transform *bios* into *zoe*!

– 68 –

Jesus wept.

John 11:35 (KJV)

Jesus wept.

John 11:35 (NIV)

This is the shortest verse in the Bible. It occurs in the context of the seventh miracle in John chapters 1–12 (seven is a number symbolic of perfection in the Jewish thought of the day). Jesus has a close friend called Lazarus who lives in Bethany, just outside Jerusalem. While Jesus is far away, He receives a message that Lazarus is gravely ill. By the time He arrives, Lazarus has been dead four days and is lying in an enclosed tomb. Jesus raises him from the dead, but before He does so John records that Jesus "wept." The original Greek verb *dakruo* is in fact stronger than that. It means "sobbed." The words "Jesus sobbed" tell us a great deal. Jesus is the one who reveals the Father. He shows us what God is really like. If Jesus weeps over Lazarus, then we know that our heavenly Father is not apathetic to our pain (like the god of the ancient Greeks) but sympathetic and even empathic. He feels what we feel. He is truly the Suffering God, "familiar with suffering" (Isa. 53:3). Whenever you feel pain as a believer, whether this is suffering you choose or suffering you don't choose, know that you have a heavenly Father who draws very close to the brokenhearted. He is not far away but near. His arms are around you. His tears mingle with yours. He is a compassionate Dad.

— 69 —

Jesus saith unto him, I am the way, the truth, and the life: no man cometh unto the Father, but by me.

John 14:6 (KJV)

Jesus answered, "I am the way and the truth and the life. No one comes to the Father except through me."

John 14:6 (NIV)

There are seven "I am" sayings of Jesus in John's Gospel: "I am the Bread of Life," "I am the Light of the World," "I am the Good Shepherd," "I am the Gate," "I am the Resurrection and the Life," "I am the Way, the Truth and the Life," and "I am the True Vine." Jesus utters the sixth of these here. He has just been teaching His disciples that He is going to leave them. This is the night before He is crucified. He tells them that He is going ahead of them to prepare a place for them in His Father's house. He then tells them that He alone is the Way to the Father, the Truth about the Father, and the Life that the Father wants to bring to the world. No one can enter a relationship with *Abba* Father except by coming to Jesus. Please notice that Jesus does not say He is "*a way*," "*a truth*," "*a life*." He uses the definite article: "*the* Way, *the* Truth, *the* Life." Jesus is unashamed of His uniqueness in the context of the world's religions. He says He is "*the* way" to the Father, not just "a way"! While it's important to have respect for the truth that you can find in other religions, sooner or later you need to come to see that it is only and exclusively through Jesus that we find our way into the Father's arms of love. Only through Jesus do we find our way back, like the prodigal son, to the Father's house.

– 70 –

I will not leave you comfortless: I will come to you.

John 14:18 (KJV)

I will not leave you as orphans; I will come to you.

John 14:18 (NIV)

It is twenty-four hours before the crucifixion. Jesus meets with His disciples and washes their feet in an extraordinary act of humility and love (John 13). Then He begins to prepare His followers for His death and departure. In John 14 the tone He strikes is one of reassurance. In verse 18, He promises His disciples that He will not leave them comfortless. The word literally means "orphans." The word "orphan" in the Hebrew Bible means "without a father." Jesus is indicating here that all human beings are without a father. He is not referring to earthly fathers—although one day we will all be orphans in this sense—but to His heavenly Father. Since the fall of Adam and Eve we have all lived in an orphan state spiritually. We have been separated from the true Father's love. However, Jesus is now about to die so that the barrier of sin can be removed and a way can be opened back to the Father. He promises the disciples that they will no longer be orphans and that He will return to them. He makes the same promise to all of us. If we choose to follow Jesus, He will make sure that we are orphans no more. We will no longer be separated from our heavenly Father's love. We will know God personally and intimately as His much-loved children.

– 71 –

Peace I leave with you, my peace I give unto you: not as the world giveth, give I unto you. Let not your heart be troubled, neither let it be afraid.

John 14:27 (KJV)

Peace I leave with you; my peace I give you. I do not give to you as the world gives. Do not let your hearts be troubled and do not be afraid.

John 14:27 (NIV)

Jesus continues speaking to His disciples in a part of John's Gospel known as "the farewell discourses" (chapters 13–17). These chapters are a record of Jesus' final teachings to His apprentices within twenty-four hours of His death on the Cross. He is seeking to bring them comfort before they witness the terrible trauma of His execution. Jesus tells His friends that He is giving them a special kind of peace. The word "peace" here is a word that was originally used to refer to the calm after a storm, the resolving of discordant musical notes, and the joining of hands in reconciliation after conflict. It harks back to the Hebrew word *shalom*, which refers to peace at every level (with God, neighbor, ourselves, and creation). Jesus says that He alone can provide this kind of peace. Nothing the world has to offer can give it. But He can. And this remains true to this day. When you choose to follow Jesus, you receive everything that He paid for at the Cross. One of the many blessings of the Cross is the Father's heavenly peace. You can't put a price tag on that. It is a serenity that the world desperately tries to achieve but which no one can find outside of Jesus.

True peace comes when you're no longer an orphan or a slave, but a son or a daughter of the world's greatest Dad.

– 72 –

Greater love hath no man than this,
that a man lay down his life for his
friends.

John 15:13 (KJV)

Greater love has no one than this, that
he lay down his life for his friends.

John 15:13 (NIV)

It was C.S. Lewis who wrote about the four great words in Classical Greek that can be translated "love." There is *phileia*, which means the love of friends. There is *storge*, which means the nurturing affection of a parent, especially a mother. There is *eros*, which means the sexual love expressed by lovers. And there is *agape*, which refers to the self-forgetful love of the one who gives up everything in the service of others. It is this fourth word that is used here in this saying in John 15. Jesus tells His disciples that there is no greater love than the *agape* love shown by someone who sacrifices his life so that his friends might live. No wonder this saying is so often used at Remembrance Sunday services as people honor the sacrifice of those who have died in war so that others might be free. But the greatest demonstration of *agape* love was on the Cross, which Jesus is anticipating in these words. This is the great ordeal awaiting Jesus in the Father's epic love story. This is the heroic moment of suffering that He is going to have to embrace. He is doing all this so that we can come to see that we aren't servants but friends. We are Jesus' friends. We are the friends of His heavenly Father. There's nothing more important than that. There's no greater honor imaginable.

− 73 −

For the Father himself loveth you,
because ye have loved me, and have
believed that I came out from God.

John 16:27 (KJV)

No, the Father himself loves you
because you have loved me and have
believed that I came from God.

John 16:27 (NIV)

Jesus now draws His farewell address to a close. He speaks openly about His return to the Father. In John's Gospel we are presented with a very clear journey: Jesus descends from the glorious realm of the Father in heaven and becomes a human being on earth. He ministers for about three years before returning to heaven at an hour appointed by the Father. This hour encompasses His death, resurrection, and ascension, which are all regarded as part of the elevation of the Son of Man (i.e. Jesus). In John 16, Jesus is now very close to leaving and He tells His disciples that everything is about to change. In their relationship to Him, they are no longer going to be servants but friends. In relation to God, the disciples are no longer going to be spiritual orphans; they are going to know that the Father loves them personally and dearly. This is all because they have chosen to love the Son and to believe that He has come from the Father. What a fantastic privilege this is, to be orphans no more, but to be the sons and daughters of such a loving Father, to be the friends of Jesus. It's simply not possible to think of any honor greater than this. And the reason we have it is because Jesus paid the price.

*And he said, Abba, Father, all things
are possible unto thee; take away this
cup from me: nevertheless not what I
will, but what thou wilt.*

Mark 14:36 (KJV)

*"Abba, Father," he said, "everything
is possible for you. Take this cup from
me. Yet not what I will, but what you
will."*

Mark 14:36 (NIV)

We have seen that Jesus' premier word for
God was *Abba*, an Aramaic word meaning
something akin to "Daddy." It was an unusual
word to use of God. Though there are hints of
the Father heart of God in the Old Testament,
no one before Jesus had dared to be so familiar, intimate, and affectionate in addressing

Almighty God. Here in Mark 14 we see Jesus in the Garden of Gethsemane on the night of His arrest and trial. He knows what lies ahead. The task the Father has given Him is almost complete. His mission to rescue the world from sin is almost done. But just as He prepares for the final twenty-four hours He finds Himself in agony of soul as He contemplates the horrors of His impending suffering. He comes to God as *Abba*, as "Daddy." He comes as a vulnerable son before an affectionate father. He wrestles with His mission with a troubled heart, asking for the cup of suffering to pass. He then submits Himself to the Father's will: "Not My will but Yours be done." The Son is truly obedient to His Father from beginning to end. In this moment of understandable trepidation, however, Jesus reveals just what agony He felt before His death—a death that had to be endured if you and I were ever to experience His Father's matchless love.

– 75 –

*And at the ninth hour Jesus cried with
a loud voice, saying, Eloi, Eloi, lama
sabachthani? which is, being inter-
preted, My God, my God, why hast
thou forsaken me?*

Mark 15:34 (KJV)

*At the ninth hour Jesus cried out in a
loud voice, "Eloi, Eloi, lama sabachthani?"—which means, "My God, my
God, why have you forsaken me?"*

Mark 15:34 (NIV)

After Jesus has prayed to His heavenly
Father, He is arrested in the Garden of Gethsemane. He endures an early morning Roman
trial in which He is condemned to death and
flogged to within an inch of His life. Jesus is
then nailed to a wooden cross on a hill known

as the Place of the Skull just outside Jerusalem. The suffering He went through must have been unimaginably extreme. Much of this would have been physical, and no doubt emotional too. But here we see the spiritual agony of Jesus as He hangs on the Cross. He cries out using words from Psalm 22 verse 1, "My God, my God, why have you abandoned me?" As Jesus takes the sin of the world on His shoulders, He becomes aware in His humanity that He no longer senses the Father's intimate presence. At this moment, He embraces all the abandonment of the orphan, human condition. He who was the Son by nature experiences abandonment so that we who are spiritual orphans might find our heart's true home in the Father's love. This is one of the greatest exchanges in history. If we can look at this act of love and not be grateful, there is something wrong. Jesus went to hell and back for you and me, all so that we might enjoy intimate communion with the Father, in this life and the life to come.

*And Jesus said unto him, Verily I say
unto thee, Today shalt thou be with me
in paradise.*

Luke 23:43 (KJV)

*Jesus answered him, "I tell you the
truth, today you will be with me in
paradise."*

Luke 23:43 (NIV)

There are seven final statements spoken
by Jesus on the Cross: "Father, forgive them,"
"You will be with Me in paradise," "Woman,
behold your son," "My God, my God, why
have You forsaken Me?" "I thirst," "It is fin-
ished," and "Father, into Your hands I commit
My spirit." Here we see the crucified Jesus
flanked by two condemned thieves. One of
them is hard-hearted and tells Jesus to save

Himself and them. The other is appalled at these words and turns to Jesus, saying, "Remember me when You come into Your kingdom." Jesus replies with this memorable saying: "Today you will be with Me in paradise." Paradise was regarded as an Eden-like garden of perfect peace, prosperity, and repose. Jesus tells the penitent criminal that not only will they be together in death; they will also be together in the life that comes after death. And there will be no waiting, nor any intermediate state of preparation. Right now, in this verse, these two men are on a bleak hill dying. In the twinkling of an eye they are going to be in a beautiful garden, alive for evermore. What a great gift Jesus has given us. Through His death on the Cross, He has made it possible for us to walk and talk with our Father in the garden, just as Adam and Eve did at the very beginning of time.

– 11 –

Jesus saith unto her, Touch me not; for I am not yet ascended to my Father: but go to my brethren, and say unto them, I ascend unto my Father, and your Father; and to my God, and your God.

John 20:17 (KJV)

Jesus said, "Do not hold on to me, for I have not yet returned to the Father. Go instead to my brothers and tell them, 'I am returning to my Father and your Father, to my God and your God.'"

John 20:17 (NIV)

This statement comes at the close of one of the most poignant scenes in the Gospels. Jesus has died and His body has been buried in a garden tomb. Two days later, in the early hours of the first Easter Sunday morning, Mary Magdalene (a female follower) goes to the tomb to weep there. She meets someone who she thinks is the gardener, but it turns out to be Jesus. He has been raised from the dead and calls her by name. At the mention of her name, Mary is overcome with joy and tries to embrace Jesus. Jesus tells her to stop holding Him, because everything has now changed in her relationship with Him and indeed with God. Her communion will now be with the Father whom Jesus has been talking about throughout His ministry. Mary, and all who follow Jesus, will now be able to relate to God as Jesus did, in an intimate, spiritual communion with *Abba* Father. With the resurrection of Jesus, it's as if the world has begun again. Now you and I can enjoy an affectionate relationship with the God and Father of our Lord Jesus Christ. Jesus has dealt with the barrier that separated us from the Father's love. Through His death and resurrection, He has shown us the way to go home.

Map of Israel in the Time of the New Testament[4]

– 78 –

*And, being assembled together with
them, [he] commanded them that they
should not depart from Jerusalem,
but wait for the promise of the Father,
which, saith he, ye have heard of me.*

Acts 1:4 (KJV)

*On one occasion, while he was eat-
ing with them, he gave them this
command: "Do not leave Jerusalem,
but wait for the gift my Father promised, which you have heard me speak
about."*

Acts 1:4 (NIV)

Momentous days followed hard after the
first Easter, when Jesus was raised from the
dead. On many occasions His disciples saw
Him alive, in His resurrection body. Over a

period of forty days, Luke the historian (the author of the Book of Acts) tells us that Jesus gave His followers many convincing proofs that He was alive. Acts 1 verse 4 describes one of these confirming encounters. Luke tells us that the risen Jesus came and met with His disciples to instruct them concerning what was about to happen. He even ate with them. As He did so, He told them to wait in Jerusalem, even though it was the city associated with so much suffering. They were to wait until the Father's promised gift arrived—the gift of the Holy Spirit. Ten days later, after Jesus had ascended to heaven in front of their very eyes, the Holy Spirit fell upon the earliest followers of Jesus and they were filled with the fire of love. When the Father promises that He is going to give us a gift, He keeps His promises. Our heavenly Father promised the gift of the Spirit to His children, and He surely delivered on that promise. Today, we can all be filled with the Holy Spirit if we choose to believe in Jesus. Our Father has promised.

— 79 —

*But ye shall receive power, after that
the Holy Ghost is come upon you: and
ye shall be witnesses unto me both in
Jerusalem, and in all Judaea, and in
Samaria, and unto the uttermost part
of the earth.*

Acts 1:8 (KJV)

*But you will receive power when the
Holy Spirit comes on you; and you will
be my witnesses in Jerusalem, and in
all Judea and Samaria, and to the ends
of the earth.*

Acts 1:8 (NIV)

Shortly before Jesus returns to His Father
in heaven, He tells His disciples that a day is
coming when they are going to be baptized
in the Holy Spirit. The word *baptize* means

to "drench." The "Holy Spirit" refers to the empowering, personal presence of God. Jesus is accordingly forewarning His apprentices that they are about to receive an overwhelming experience of the Father's love and power in their lives. This experience will be totally immersive; it will inspire them to be brave witnesses to the resurrection of Jesus. This is what the earliest Christians received, and indeed what every Christian since is to receive—an empowerment of the Holy Spirit that enables us to communicate the good news about Jesus locally, regionally, nationally, and globally. This is the task of the church. The church is not a social club full of nice people who do good works. It is a courageous band of heralds proclaiming the Lordship of Jesus in Spirit-empowered words. With the fire of God's love burning in our hearts, all things are possible. We can speak the message of the Father's love with confidence, both in our words and in our actions, both where we live and in all the places where we set our feet.

− 80 −

This Jesus hath God raised up, whereof we all are witnesses.

Acts 2:32 (KJV)

God has raised this Jesus to life, and we are all witnesses of the fact.

Acts 2:32 (NIV)

After the Holy Spirit falls upon the 120 disciples in Jerusalem, Simon Peter stands up to speak. He begins to give his first sermon to a huge crowd in the city of Jerusalem. He is bold in speaking about the fire that has just fallen, telling his listeners that all this is in fulfilment of what the prophet Joel predicted about God pouring out His Spirit on all flesh. He is then equally bold in preaching about Jesus— the Jesus who ministered in Israel, who died on the Cross, who rose from the dead, who ascended into heaven, and who is both Messiah and Lord. Peter tells his listeners that Jesus is risen and alive and that he and others are all witnesses to that fact. No counter argument is brought forward, because there is none. All those in Jerusalem at the time knew that Peter had witnessed Jesus raised from the dead, and they couldn't argue with his testimony. Peter's boldness wins the crowd over. The Peter who denied Jesus a matter of weeks before is now bravely proclaiming Him. Only something life-changing could have done that to Peter. That "something" is the gift that the Father promised—the empowering presence of the Holy Spirit in the lives of all those who put their trust in Jesus. With that fire burning in the hearth of our hearts, we confidently share about what the Father has done for us.

– 81 –

For I am not ashamed of the gospel of Christ: for it is the power of God unto salvation to every one that believeth; to the Jew first, and also to the Greek.

Romans 1:16 (KJV)

I am not ashamed of the gospel, because it is the power of God for the salvation of everyone who believes: first for the Jew, then for the Gentile.

Romans 1:16 (NIV)

The greatest event in the New Testament outside the Gospels is without doubt the conversion of Saul of Tarsus. Saul had been persecuting the church. He had been responsible for the arrest and execution of Christians. He was feared among the members of the earliest church. But then the Father turned his life upside down. Saul had an encounter with the risen Jesus on the road to Damascus. This changed his life and his name. He became Paul the apostle. Here Paul tells us that he is unashamed of proclaiming the gospel of Christ. In the ancient world, "gospel" was a word used for the announcement of a Roman military victory somewhere in the empire—a victory that established *Pax Romana*, the Roman rule of peace. In the New Testament it is used to describe the Christian's declaration that Christ has vanquished the evil powers of this universe and has established God's rule of peace. Paul's gospel is the gospel not of Caesar but of Christ. When it is heard and believed, it has the power to transform human lives completely. And this gospel is inclusive—it is for everyone, Jew and Gentile. This is because the Father has had a plan right from the beginning. As He promised Abraham, the Father's blessing was to reach all nations. His love is for everyone, whatever their race or background.

– 82 –

*For ye have not received the spirit
of bondage again to fear; but ye
have received the Spirit of adoption,
whereby we cry, Abba, Father.*

Romans 8:15 (KJV)

*For you did not receive a spirit that
makes you a slave again to fear, but
you received the Spirit of sonship. And
by him we cry, "Abba, Father."*

Romans 8:15 (NIV)

Paul is writing to the Roman Christians here. He has just been telling them that they should not live according to the inclinations of their sinful flesh. They should live lives led by the Holy Spirit. He makes the point that those who are led by the Spirit of God are the sons of God. In other words, those who are truly in relationship with the Father allow the Holy Spirit to direct their choices and their conduct. He then proceeds to tell them that they really are sons (and of course daughters) of God. They have been rescued and redeemed from slavery and they have been adopted by the Father through the death of Jesus Christ. They now have the Spirit at work within their hearts (see Rom. 5:5), and this Spirit is the one whom John Wesley called "the loving Spirit of Adoption." This Spirit ignites our hearts with the flame of love and enables us to call God *Abba*, or Daddy. While Jesus is the One and Only Son by nature, we who believe in Jesus are the sons and daughters of God by adoption. With the Spirit of adoption in our hearts, we are moved to call God our Papa, our Father, our Daddy. This is what worship is— responding to the overtures of the Father's love by crying out to God, in the Holy Spirit, that He's the best Dad in the universe and most worthy of our highest praise.

– 83 –

The Spirit itself beareth witness with our spirit, that we are the children of God.

Romans 8:16 (KJV)

The Spirit himself testifies with our spirit that we are God's children.

Romans 8:16 (NIV)

Here Paul speaks about the role of the Holy Spirit in our adoption. Paul has in mind the Roman practice of adoption (which he would have seen) in which a couple would approach one of their slaves and ask to adopt their son. The slave would invariably say yes, because his child would be rescued from a very dangerous and impoverished life. When the exchange happened, it followed a process in which the natural father sold his boy three times to the adopting father. All this would be done in the presence of seven witnesses before being signed by a Roman magistrate. The magistrate would ask these witnesses if the adoption process had been formally completed. They would confirm this, and the slave's child would become the son of a freeman, with all the new privileges that came with his new status as the new father's son and heir. Here Paul tells us that the Holy Spirit is the witness of our adoption. He testifies in our spirits that we are the adopted children of God. He is the love of the Father poured out in our hearts (see Rom. 5:5). With the fire of the Spirit burning in us, we will always have a witness to the fact that we are the adopted children of the living God, that we are co-heirs with Jesus, and that our future is secure just as our inheritance is sure.

– 84 –

For the earnest expectation of the creature waiteth for the manifestation of the sons of God.

Romans 8:19 (KJV)

The creation waits in eager expectation for the sons of God to be revealed.

Romans 8:19 (NIV)

In the timeframe between the first coming of Jesus and His second coming (on the last day of history), Paul teaches that the whole of creation is groaning like a woman in labor pains. There is a longing throughout the earth for the Son to return and for this fallen universe to be recreated as the new heavens and the new earth. As creation waits, it does so with "eager expectation." The word here is used of someone straining on tiptoe to see something ahead on the distant horizon. Paul of course is speaking here figuratively, not literally. He doesn't regard creation as a literal, living soul. But he does regard creation as frustrated in its fallen state, forever falling into decay, and he sees it as expectant for that day when the Father's adopted sons and daughters will be revealed. When that happens, the world will enter the fulfilment of all its longings. Then the planet will hear Jesus say, "Behold, I make all things new!" No wonder then that the entire creation is waiting, groaning, and anticipating the day when the true sons and daughters of God will appear on the earth. This is the Father's endgame—that there will come a time when everyone who believes in Jesus is so filled with the Spirit of adoption that they bring true freedom not only to enslaved people but to an enslaved planet. That is some adventure!

– 85 –

*For I am persuaded, that neither death,
nor life, nor angels, nor principalities,
nor powers, nor things present, nor
things to come, nor height, nor depth,
nor any other creature, shall be able
to separate us from the love of God,
which is in Christ Jesus our Lord.*

Romans 8:38–39 (KJV)

*For I am convinced that neither death
nor life, neither angels nor demons,
neither the present nor the future, nor
any powers, neither height nor depth,
nor anything else in all creation, will be
able to separate us from the love of
God that is in Christ Jesus our Lord.*

Romans 8:38–39 (NIV)

Romans chapter 8 is one of the greatest chapters of the Bible. It begins with Paul announcing that there is no condemnation for those who are in Christ Jesus. It ends with him declaring that there is no separation for those who are in relationship with Christ. What kind of separation is Paul referring to here? He is talking about separation from the Father's love. This separation between the Father and all human beings has come to an end in the glorious death and resurrection of Jesus Christ. The first Adam's sin had caused this separation, but now a Second Adam—Jesus Christ—has come and paid the penalty for sin on the Cross. Now there is nothing that can ever separate a true believer from the Father's love revealed in Jesus Christ. Paul is utterly convinced that this is true. The millennia of separation have ended. A new age has dawned. A new creation has occurred, and now those who are "in Christ" will never again be separated from the Father's love.

— 86 —

For I am persuaded, that neither death, nor life, nor angels, nor principalities, nor powers, nor things present, nor things to come, nor height, nor depth, nor any other creature, shall be able to separate us from the love of God, which is in Christ Jesus our Lord.

Romans 8:38-39 (KJV)

For I am convinced that neither death nor life, neither angels nor demons, neither the present nor the future, nor any powers, neither height nor depth, nor anything else in all creation, will be able to separate us from the love of God that is in Christ Jesus our Lord.

Romans 8:38-39 (NIV)

Romans chapter 8 is one of the most uplifting chapters in the entire Bible. The apostle Paul begins by saying that there is no condemnation for the person who is in a living relationship with the Lord Jesus. What does this mean? That there is no divine judgment for their sin. This is good news indeed! We might even ask, could the news get any better than this? The answer is yes! If the chapter begins by reassuring us that there is no condemnation by the Father, the end of Romans 8 says something equally if not more beautiful—that there is no separation from the Father's love either.

You see the design here? There is no condemnation (at the beginning of Romans 8) and no separation (the end of Romans 8). For anyone who has experienced rupture in their attachment to their father, this is deeply reassuring. We may become orphans in this life, but we will not become orphans in the life to come. We may have experienced the agony of being separated from our earthly father, but we will never experience this in relation to our heavenly Father. This Father will never forsake us and there is nothing in either the spiritual or the earthly realm that can change that fact. Once we are in relationship with Jesus, we will never be separated from the Father's love ever again. Once you begin to know this in your heart, you will no longer live out of a center of fear; you will live from a center of love. You will know that the Father's love never fails, and it never gives up. Wow!

– 87 –

Though I speak with the tongues of men and of angels, and have not charity, I am become as sounding brass, or a tinkling cymbal.

1 Corinthians 13:1 (KJV)

If I speak in the tongues of men and of angels, but have not love, I am only a resounding gong or a clanging cymbal.

1 Corinthians 13:1 (NIV)

First Corinthians 13 is one of the best-known chapters in the Bible. It is a fine passage in praise of true love and for that reason is often read at weddings. Here Paul is writing to the church in Corinth and he is teaching them about how to use the gifts of the Spirit wisely—supernatural gifts such as speaking in tongues, prophesying, and performing miracles. More than excelling in such gifts, Paul urges his readers to excel in love for one another. The King James Version renders the Greek word *agape* "charity." Today we would call it "self-sacrificial love." This is the Christian's characteristic and unique word for love. Here in verse 1 Paul says that no language, either earthly or heavenly, can compare with the practice of Christlike love. "If I speak eloquently or speak in tongues, and I do not excel in self-giving love, then I'm nothing but an echoing gong or clanging metal." This is what the Father has been longing for since the beginning of time—a people who are so filled with His love and kindness that they simply cannot resist giving it away, not only to fellow Christians but to those outside the church as well. Just as the Father is characterized by love, so His sons and daughters are to be characterized by it too. We are to walk in the Father's love and give it away.

— 88 —

And [I] will be a Father unto you, and ye shall be my sons and daughters, saith the Lord Almighty.

2 Corinthians 6:18 (KJV)

I will be a Father to you, and you will be my sons and daughters, says the Lord Almighty.

2 Corinthians 6:18 (NIV)

Second Corinthians is a letter in which Paul really wears his heart on his sleeve. Here he implores his readers not to have anything to do with people who lead them astray but to separate themselves from them. At the end of the chapter he strings together three quotations from the Old Testament with the intention of showing that God longs for intimate communion with them, but that this intimacy is dependent upon their purity. In the last of the three, Paul quotes a prophecy given to King David in 2 Samuel 7:14. The promise is for David's son Solomon, as we saw earlier in this little book. "I will be a father to him, and he will be My son." Paul now relates this prophecy to his readers and has the Father saying to them, "You will be My sons." Paul also adds "and My daughters." God longs to be a

Father to both men and women. He wants an affectionate relationship with both daughters and sons. Perhaps no verse sums up the love story of the entire Bible better than this. Right from the beginning of all things, the Father has set His heart on creating a loving family in which Jesus is His Son by nature, and we who believe in Jesus are His sons and daughters by adoption. This is the purpose of the entire story of the Bible.

— 89 —

Having predestinated us unto the adoption of children by Jesus Christ to himself, according to the good pleasure of his will.

Ephesians 1:5 (KJV)

*He predestined us to be adopted as
his sons through Jesus Christ, in accordance with his pleasure and will.*

Ephesians 1:5 (NIV)

The letter to the Ephesians begins with a magnificent prayer of thanksgiving. The author starts this by saying, "Blessed be the God and Father of our Lord Jesus Christ." He then goes on to thank the Father for all the blessings we have "in Christ." The first thing he mentions is in verses 4 and 5. He praises God for choosing a people to be His own before the world was even made. He talks about how the Father predestined us and says that this was for adoption into His family. The author here was thinking of the Roman practice of adoption—a process in which the son of a slave was bought out of servitude and placed in a new family, with a new father. All previous debts were cancelled, and the adopted son became the heir to his new parents' fortune. That is some transformation!

The author uses this as a picture to describe how followers of Jesus have been given a brand-new Father and a brand-new family. This plan of adoption gave *Abba* Father great pleasure and joy. It continues to fill Him with delight today. The important thing is to realize that His invitation to become part of His family is open to everyone. No one is too poor, too shameful, too dirty, too lost to receive this gift. Including you and me.

– 90 –

For we are his workmanship, created in Christ Jesus unto good works, which God hath before ordained that we should walk in them.

Ephesians 2:10 (KJV)

For we are God's workmanship, created in Christ Jesus to do good works, which God prepared in advance for us to do.

Ephesians 2:10 (NIV)

This verse comes at the end of a passage in which Paul tells us how we have been saved by grace. Grace is the undeserved love and the empowering presence of Jesus in our lives. Good works on our part did not secure our salvation from sin. What Jesus did at the Cross has achieved that. What we are called to do for our part is put our faith in Christ's amazing grace. We are called to believe that Jesus has paid the price for our sins. Then we will be saved from a life of gratifying the desires of our sinful nature. And we will not only be rescued *from* something. We will be rescued *to* something as well—a life of doing the good works that the Father has prepared in advance for us to do. We are accordingly not saved *by* good works, but we are saved *to* good works. And when we are saved, we become God's workmanship. The word in

Greek is *poema*, from which we get our word "poem." As redeemed sons and daughters, we are the Father's masterpieces! We are His paintings, His sculptures, His poetry, His songs, His symphonies, His works of art. However low your self-image is right now, understand that heaven thinks highly of you and you are the apple of the Father's eye.

— 91 —

Put on the whole armour of God, that ye may be able to stand against the wiles of the devil.

Ephesians 6:11 (KJV)

Put on the full armor of God so that you can take your stand against the devil's schemes.

Ephesians 6:11 (NIV)

Paul knows that as Christians we are engaged in a ferocious spiritual war between light and darkness. On the Cross, Jesus Christ has conquered the dark forces of this universe. Though Satan has been defeated through the death and resurrection of Jesus, he still fights on and will continue to do so until the last day of history, when he is finally destroyed. In the meantime, Christians are called to fight the good fight. We are not left ill-equipped or alone in this war. We are given the mighty power of the Holy Spirit. We are also given items of spiritual armor. Thinking of the Roman legionaries of his own day, Paul lists the items of our spiritual armor: a breastplate (righteousness), a belt (truth), shoes (peace), a helmet (salvation), a shield (faith), and a sword (God's Word). With these resources we become part of the Father's army, eradicating evil not with the love of power but with the power of love. We are Dad's army. We are sons and daughters committed to bringing heaven to those who are experiencing hell on earth. In this battle, we must know our identity—we are sons and daughters of the High King of Heaven. We must also know our authority; there is mighty power in the name of Jesus. When you know who you are, you also know what you have, and this makes you a real threat to the enemy!

– 92 –

Now faith is the substance of things hoped for, the evidence of things not seen.

Hebrews 11:1 (KJV)

Faith is being sure of what we hope for and certain of what we do not see.

Hebrews 11:1 (NIV)

Have you ever wondered what faith is? In this verse from the letter to the Hebrews, the author gives one of the best definitions you'll ever find. He says that faith is the act of believing that what you cannot yet see is real. Christians believe that Jesus Christ is real, that He exists, that He is what the first Christians claimed Him to be. They believe that He is risen from the dead and alive for evermore. They cannot yet see Jesus physically. But one day they will when He returns to the earth on the clouds and in magnificent glory. This act of believing requires that we put our trust in something (or, better still, someone) invisible. While there is plenty of reasonable, historical evidence that Jesus rose from the dead, in the end it is an act of faith to believe that Jesus is alive today. The reward of believing is that we eventually see the one whom we have believed in. The Bible teaches that Jesus Christ will return at the end of history. On that day, all those who have been certain of what they haven't seen will see Him. So, while sceptics say, "I'll believe it when I see it," the Christian says, "I'll see it when I believe it." This is what faith is, and no one can ever become a Christian without believing in their hearts that

Jesus is risen from the dead, that He is alive, and that He is Lord!

– 93 –

Pure religion and undefiled before God and the Father is this, To visit the fatherless and widows in their affliction, and to keep himself unspotted from the world.

James 1:27 (KJV)

Religion that God our Father accepts as pure and faultless is this: to look after orphans and widows in their distress and to keep oneself from being polluted by the world.

James 1:27 (NIV)

The letter of James stresses that a person whose faith is "alive" will do good works for the Father. James nowhere says that we are saved from our sins by good works. That would put all the credit for our salvation in our hands. But James does teach us that we are saved *unto* good works. In other words, once a person is saved and adopted into the Father's family, they will inevitably seek to do the Father's will, to do the work that the Father asks them to do. One of the clearest descriptions of the kind of good works that James has in mind is in this verse. Here we learn what kind of religion the Father accepts as real—when believers care for the two groups of people for whom the Father has a special affection: orphans and widows. Until the return of Jesus Christ, Christians are to busy themselves with showing compassion in practical ways to the wounded and the brokenhearted. To do that, Christians must keep themselves from being defiled by the selfish values of a fallen world. As sons and daughters of a loving Father, Christians show that they are truly the Father's children by seeking to reverse the curse of fatherlessness on the earth. This is what living faith looks like; it isn't just a matter of believing in Jesus so that we'll go to heaven when we die; it's believing in Jesus in order to bring heaven to earth while we live.

— 94 —

For the Lord himself shall descend from heaven with a shout, with the voice of the archangel, and with the trump of God: and the dead in Christ shall rise first.

1 Thessalonians 4:16 (KJV)

For the Lord himself will come down from heaven, with a loud command, with the voice of the archangel and

*with the trumpet call of God, and the
dead in Christ will rise first.*

1 Thessalonians 4:16 (NIV)

According to the New Testament, history is marching toward a momentous climax. It will begin with the return of Jesus on the last day. When this happens, there will be a noise enough to wake the dead—literally. There will be a loud command, the voice of the archangel, and the trumpet call of God! The loud command is like the shout of an officer to his troops. In this context it refers to Jesus issuing the order for the dead to rise. This command will be accompanied by the Archangel (most likely Michael) sounding God's trumpet. In the Old Testament, when God came down to meet His people it was sometimes accompanied by a trumpet blast (see Exod. 19:16). Imagine a deafening, reverberating sound throughout the universe as Jesus comes back. The Lord's return will accordingly be audible as well as visible. Those who have died in

Christ will rise to meet Jesus first. They will be followed by those who are still alive and who know the Lord. This is the final act of the Father's epic story, revealed in the pages of the Bible. The same Jesus who ascended to the heavens two thousand years ago will descend from the heavens at some point in the years to come. The story of the world does not therefore head toward a hopeless end, but rather toward an endless hope.

– 95 –

Let no man deceive you by any means: for that day shall not come, except there come a falling away first, and that man of sin be revealed, the son of perdition.

2 Thessalonians 2:3 (KJV)

Don't let anyone deceive you in any way, for that day will not come until the rebellion occurs and the man of lawlessness is revealed, the man doomed to destruction.

2 Thessalonians 2:3 (NIV)

In every great story, the final act often involves a dark night and a final battle. The Bible tells the Father's story of human history, and in this story too there is intense darkness and conflict before the conclusion. Before Jesus returns, there will be a period of extreme turmoil on the earth known as the Great Tribulation. This will involve a worldwide rebellion. This rebellion will be the final attempt of the enemy—the devil—to tempt human beings into an orphan-hearted independence from the Father. Paul says the "day" (namely the day of the Son's return) will not happen until a global falling away of half-hearted believers has occurred. He adds that a "man of lawlessness" will appear in that time, a man "doomed to destruction." Lawlessness is the logical outcome of the orphan state. Satan is the ultimate orphan, so this man of lawlessness is a human being utterly opposed to the Father and the Son. He is a shameless blasphemer against God. He is the Anti-Christ. He will have a period of dominance on the world scene, but at the return of Jesus he will be completely defeated and destroyed. Every human being will have a choice as the end draws near and as the world descends into moral anarchy and political chaos; will we submit to the father of lies (the devil) or the Father of lights (God)?

— 96 —

Love not the world, neither the things that are in the world. If any man love the world, the love of the Father is not in him.

1 John 2:15 (KJV)

Do not love the world or anything in the world. If anyone loves the world, the love of the Father is not in him.

1 John 2:15 (NIV)

Here John sets up a contrast. Every day, Christians must choose between loving the world and loving the Father. What we are talking about here is unhealthy and healthy attachment. You can choose to be attached to the things that this world has to offer. This is toxic. Or, you can choose to be attached to the Father's love. This is spiritual, mental, emotional health. What the world has to offer is nothing in comparison with what *Abba* Father has to offer. The world traps us in the enticing but deadly grip of addiction, specifically addiction to the idols of money, sex, and power. This is a completely distorted and perverted use of the worship drive that is part of our God-given wiring. It is, in short, idolatry. But there is a better way to express our will to worship. The Father draws us with cords of love into a relationship in which we are seized by the power of the greatest affection of all—the love of the Father. This causes us to want to cry out, "God, You're my perfect Father! You're the world's greatest Dad!" While the world fills the hole in the soul with the worship of idols, Christians ask the Father to saturate their hearts with liquid waves of love. Those who are the children of God are accordingly to live in a state of detachment from this world and in a state of attachment to the love that the world is looking for in all the wrong places. This is what John meant by choosing "the love of the Father" over love for the world or anything in the world.

– 97 –

Behold, what manner of love the Father hath bestowed upon us, that we should be called the sons of God: therefore the world knoweth us not, because it knew him not.

1 John 3:1 (KJV)

How great is the love the Father has lavished on us, that we should be called children of God! And that is what we are! The reason the world does not know us is that it did not know him.

1 John 3:1 (NIV)

John captures our attention with the little word "look" or "behold." He goes on to ask, "What kind of love is this?" He is referring to the Father's love—a love that created the world and a love that has now redeemed the world in Christ. John becomes eloquent and lyrical about this love. He says that the Father has bestowed upon us the Love of all loves. In fact, the word "bestowed" is a little weak. The verb does not just mean "granted." It means "lavished," as the New International Version renders it. The Father has poured His affections out upon us, and the proof is that we have now become the children of God. We have become sons and daughters by adoption. The world does not recognize these sons and daughters, but then the world didn't recognize the Son, Jesus, either. How wonderful it is to be loved by the world's greatest Father! This love is not given in paltry portions. No, we have a Father who loves us extravagantly, outrageously, immeasurably. This means that we should never come to God as orphans, frightened that He will not give us any more of

His love if we hold out our hands and plead to Him. It's quite the opposite. We have a heavenly Father who doesn't just bestow His love; He lavishes it on us! Let's renounce once and forever the timid, uncertain, insecure heart of the orphan and replace it with the confident, trusting and secure love of a son or a daughter. Let's celebrate with John and cry out, "How great is this love!"

— 98 —

There is no fear in love; but perfect love casteth out fear: because fear hath torment. He that feareth is not made perfect in love.

1 John 4:18 (KJV)

There is no fear in love. But perfect love drives out fear, because fear has

*to do with punishment. The one who
fears is not made perfect in love.*

1 John 4:18 (NIV)

One of the great themes of the first letter
of John is assurance—especially assurance of
a believer's salvation from sin and of our status as sons and daughters of the High King of
Heaven. Here John sets up a striking contrast
between two states of mind—being afraid
and being loved. He says that Christians
are not to be afraid. We are not to be fear-
ful, like orphans and slaves. No, we are sons
and daughters. As such, we are to live from
a center of love, not from a center of fear.
What do orphans and slaves fear? They fear
being punished. John is here referring to the
fear of being punished for our sins at the Last
Judgment at the very end of history. Make no
mistake, we live in a moral universe, and one
day there will be a reckoning for what human
beings have done with their lives and in their
lives. But Christians are not to live in fear that

God will condemn them. Jesus has taken their punishment at Calvary. Any judgment that was coming to them has been absorbed by the crucified body of Jesus. Christians are therefore to know that they are dearly loved—eternally loved by *Abba* Father, who will never condemn them. This love expels fear. As the end of history draws nearer, Christians are more and more called to live in the assurance of the Father's love, not in toxic fear. This love perfects them—it makes them whole, complete, and at peace.

— 99 —

And I saw the dead, small and great, stand before God; and the books were opened: and another book was opened, which is the book of life: and the dead were judged out of those

*things which were written in the books,
according to their works.*

Revelation 20:12 (KJV)

*And I saw the dead, great and small,
standing before the throne, and
books were opened. Another book
was opened, which is the book of life.
The dead were judged according to
what they had done as recorded in the
books.*

Revelation 20:12 (NIV)

The Bible teaches that there are four final events that await the world at the end of time: (1) the return of Jesus Christ, (2) the resurrection of all dead people (sometimes known as the General Resurrection), (3) the last judgment, and (4) the creation of the new heavens and the new earth. In Revelation 20, Satan has just been thrown into the lake of fire. He is now finally, completely defeated and destroyed. The orphan-maker can do no more harm and reap no more havoc on planet earth. Now, before the great white throne, the last judgment begins. All are judged, both the great (in the world's eyes) and the small. God has two books: a record of all our deeds and the book of life. This is a reminder that we write our own destinies in this life. We must choose today to step out of our orphan state and live as sons and daughters of God. The Father knows His children. Their names are engraved upon His hand and written in His book forever. As you come to the end of this little book about the Father's great story, told in the Bible, the most important thing you can do is make sure your name is written in the Father's book of everlasting Life. You do this by first repenting of your sins and believing in Jesus, and second by living as a faithful son or daughter of God for the rest of your life.

— 100 —

*And God shall wipe away all tears from
their eyes; and there shall be no more
death, neither sorrow, nor crying, neither shall there be any more pain: for
the former things are passed away.*

Revelation 21:4 (KJV)

*He will wipe every tear from their eyes.
There will be no more death or mourn-
ing or crying or pain, for the old order
of things has passed away.*

Revelation 21:4 (NIV)

When all is said and done, and the new
heavens and the new earth have been created
out of our existing heavens and earth, there
will be a final great display of the Father's
love. From heaven, the Father, the Son, and
the Holy Spirit will come to this renewed

creation and make their home with us. A city will descend from heaven—a city where there will be no more suffering, no more crying, no more pain, and no more dying. Here, in a city without a cemetery, the Father will come to us and look into our eyes with indescribable compassion. He will wipe away all our tears. Our orphan hearts will be healed. And in His gaze, a thousand painful memories will disappear like the mist of a new dawn. It will be the happiest and most glorious of days. And it will not be the end of the adventure. It will be just the beginning. So, as this story ends, let your own story begin. You have read a summary of the Father's story in this little book—the story of the history of the world, from the prologue to the epilogue, from Genesis to Revelation. What part are you going to play in this epic drama? Are you going to play a bit part on the side of those lost in darkness? Or are you going to begin your own hero's journey, siding with the light, so filled with the Father's love that you cannot resist giving it away to others for the rest of your life? The choice is yours. Choose wisely, my friend.

a LOVE LETTER from our FATHER

Based on the 100 verses in this book

My beloved child

Even before the foundations of the world I was thinking of you

I created the heavens and the earth as your home, and I made you in My own image

I created your frame and breathed life into your soul

All this I did out of love so that I could be your Father and you could be My child

Even though My children chose to depart from Me, I have never forgotten them, and I have never forgotten you

My plan has always been to rescue My wayward sons and daughters

Because My love is a promise-keeping, covenant love

I promised Abraham that through him I would bless every nation under the sun

And when Israel was in Egypt, oppressed by Pharaoh, I raised up Moses to deliver My people

For My people are My adopted children, My very own

I led them toward a land flowing with milk and honey

Like a father carrying a child upon his shoulders

I made them a kingdom of priests and a holy nation

I promised I would bless them if they kept My laws

For I am compassionate and gracious

Slow to anger

Abounding in love and faithfulness

And I am jealous for those whom I call My children

I smile upon those who obey Me

I said to My people of old what I say to you today

Be strong and very courageous

For I am with you

I am your Father

My goodness and mercy follow you all

the days of your life

And you will one day live in My house forever

When others forsake you, I will not

When earthly fathers and mothers abandon you, I will hold you close

For I am the Father to the fatherless

The defender of the cause of widows

And the one who has compassion on His children

For I knew you before you were born

I formed you in your mother's womb

All your days were written down in My Book of Life before you took your first breath

And I long to give you the desires of your heart

So trust in Me

Even a mighty flood could never drown the love that I have for you

I am always ready to hear, to forgive, and to heal

Even when you feel all alone, I am there

I am your everlasting Father

And you are the work of My hands

I rejoice over you with singing

And I quiet you with My love

For I know the plans that I have for you, and My plans are good

They are to prosper you, not to harm you

All I ask is that you let Me write My law upon your hearts

Because I want to put a new spirit within you

And turn your heart of stone to a heart of flesh

I want to reveal My secrets to you

And to give you My Holy Spirit as your helper

Do not grieve, for My joy is your strength

I sent My Son Jesus into the world to give you My peace

He is the Lord of the heavens and the earth

Yet He was born as a baby

He came and dwelt among you

I declared Him to be My beloved Son, the pride of My life

And appointed Him to usher in My reign on the earth

He is the one who truly transforms the human soul

Listen to Him

Learn to speak to Me as your dearest Father

And seek as My children to bring heaven to earth

Ask Me for what you need in this task

And do all that you do from a place of rest and security in My love

Live as little children before Me

Do not pursue worldly idols

But put Me first in your life

I want to show you My compassion and affection

As only a perfect father can

I loved you so much that I sent My one and only Son

That you might live forever with Me

Everything you need you can only find in My Son

For He came to bring you life— abundant life

He alone reveals My Father heart

He alone is the Way to My love

I sent Him so that you would no longer be a spiritual orphan

And so that your heart would not be troubled again

He laid down His life for you

So that you would know that I love you dearly

He drank the cup of deepest sorrow

Embraced the pain of absolute desolation

So that all your sins might be forgiven

And so that you and I could enjoy paradise together

Because of what My Son did on the Cross

You can know Me as He knows Me

As your Father

I sent My Holy Spirit just as I promised

So that your heart would be captured by My love

And your mouth would speak of My Son

Be bold as a witness of My love

Do not be ashamed of the good news of My Son

For I have delivered you from fear

And adopted you out of My great love

So that you might call Me Abba, Daddy

So that you would be sure that you are Mine

And I am yours

So, take My love to this broken world

The whole of creation is waiting for you

Nothing that opposes you will ever separate you from My love

For My love is patient and kind

My love is self-giving and eternal

Ever since the world began

My plan has been to say to you

"I am your Father"

I predestined you for your adoption

*And the thought of that made Me
smile with joy*

You are My poetry

You are My song

You are My masterpiece

You are My work of art

I have prepared an assignment for you

*Put on My armor and fight for the
cause of My love*

Stand firm against the Adversary

For his days are numbered

*Believe in Me even though you cannot
yet see Me*

And take My love to the orphan and the widow

All this I call you to do until the final day

When out of heaven My Son will come

And the dead will be raised

Though there may be great trouble before that day

Hold fast to your love for Me

For I have lavished My love on you

And I will always lavish My love on you

When the storm clouds begin to gather in the world

Rest in My perfect love

And do not be afraid

For My Son is coming soon

And He will judge the earth

The enemy will be no more

There will be no more tears

And you and I will be face to face in the end

Just as it was in the beginning

I am your Father

You are My child

I love you

And I will never stop loving you

With endless love,

From

Abba, Father

ENDNOTES

1. The Ten Commandments https://en.wikipedia.org/wiki
   /Moses#/media/File:Philippe_de_Champaigne_-_Moses
   _with_the_Ten_Commandments_-_WGA04717.jpg

2. Canaan and the Twelve Tribes of Israel (Joshua 14)
   https://commons.wikimedia.org/wiki/File:12_Tribes_of
   _Israel_Map.svg

3. Division of the Two Kingdoms https://commons.wikimedia
   .org/wiki/File:Kingdoms_of_Israel_and_Judah_map_830-es
   .svg#/media/File:Kingdoms_of_Israel_and_Judah_map_830
   .svg

4. Map of Israel in the Time of the New Testament Palestine in
   the Time of Christ https://www.sacred-texts.com/bib/maps
   /img/006.jpg

about MARK STIBBE

Described by the New York Times as an "acclaimed Christian author," Dr. Mark Stibbe has written over forty books, including *God's Word for Every Need*. Lately, he has also taken to writing and publishing novels, including his Christmas story, *King of Hearts*. He leads regular workshops on writing and storytelling, and along with his wife Cherith runs BookLab, a business dedicated to helping good writers become great authors. Contact him at www.advice4authors.com.

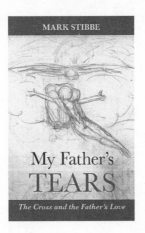

MARK STIBBE

My Father's
TEARS

The Cross and the Father's Love

for FURTHER READING

If you want to go deeper into the Father's story told in the Bible, then Mark Stibbe's book *My Father's Tears* is essential reading. Published by SPCK, London, this tells the story of the Father's passionate love for the world He made and the human beings He created. It is a beautiful book that will illuminate your mind and warm your heart.

What reviewers have said:

"This book offers a real key to our understanding of how an orphan generation may know the healing power of a
Father's love."

"This is one of the profoundest, poetic,
poignant and prophetic books that ever
read me! It spoke deeply to both mind
and spirit."

"Brilliant book, reaffirming just how much
the Father loves us, how closely He
walks with us and how if we want an
accurate picture of God we should look
to Jesus."

"A superb book."

•

Experience a personal revival!

Spirit-empowered content from today's top Christian authors delivered directly to your inbox.

Join today!
lovetoreadclub.com

Inspiring Articles
Powerful Video Teaching
Resources for Revival

Get all of this and so much more, e-mailed to you twice weekly!

LOVE TO READ CLUB
by **D DESTINY IMAGE**